T0291417

# Reflexive Leadership in Context

This concise textbook seeks to unpack the real-life complexities of leadership by examining the theories and models surrounding it and encouraging self-analysis in the individual's own contexts.

The book:

- Provides an outline of the various perspectives of leadership theory;
- Develops a critical and robust framework for considering existing leadership theory and consequently applying leadership practice across the organization;
- Identifies important individual characteristics likely to enhance leadership practice in the workplace;
- Considers a framework for analyzing leadership performance and methods and practicalities for application.

*Reflexive Leadership in Context* provides a practical and concise introduction for executive education students currently studying for MSc/MBA apprenticeship programs, as well as supplementary reading for postgraduate students studying modules within leadership and management.

**Paul Evans** is Lecturer in Leadership and Management Development at the Alliance Manchester Business School, Manchester, UK.

# Management Practice Essentials

This series of shortform textbooks has been developed to align with and support the Level 7 Senior Leader Master's Degree Apprenticeship (SLMDA). Each book concentrates on a key element of the SLMDA Standard and therefore covers a core essential of management practice. The series is centred around critical reflection on the underlying assumptions the individual leader or manager might make and their current practice, and collectively designed to enhance leadership knowledge, skills and behaviours. An ideal approach for any executive education course delivered through blended learning, and a useful alternative or supplement to traditional textbooks for a range of postgraduate Business & Management modules, the books:

- Combine theory and practice – providing students with knowledge and critical understanding of the theories, concepts and principles of leading organisations and focusing on the practical application and execution of these concepts;
- Are experience-led – providing students with the opportunity to develop their intellectual, practical and transferable skills and behaviours necessary to successfully analyse, develop and manage organisations.
- Include features to aid learning and understanding, such as chapter objectives, summaries, reflective questions and additional PowerPoint slides and cases available online.

**Reflexive Leadership in Context**
*Paul Evans*

For more information about the series, please visit www.routledge.com/ Management-Practice-Essentials/book-series/MPE

# Reflexive Leadership in Context

**Paul Evans**

Routledge
Taylor & Francis Group

LONDON AND NEW YORK

First published 2021
by Routledge
2 Park Square, Milton Park, Abingdon, Oxon OX14 4RN

and by Routledge
52 Vanderbilt Avenue, New York, NY 10017

*Routledge is an imprint of the Taylor & Francis Group, an informa business*

*British Library Cataloguing-in-Publication Data*
A catalogue record for this book is available from the British Library

*Library of Congress Cataloging-in-Publication Data*
Names: Evans, Paul, 1963– author.
Title: Reflexive leadership in context / Paul Evans.
Description: New York : Routledge, 2021. | Series: Management practice essentials | Includes bibliographical references and index.
Identifiers: LCCN 2020027088 (print) | LCCN 2020027089 (ebook) | ISBN 9780367511166 (hardback) | ISBN 9781003052470 (ebook)
Subjects: LCSH: Leadership—Psychological aspects. | Management. | Business planning.
Classification: LCC HD57.7 .E853 2021 (print) | LCC HD57.7 (ebook) | DDC 658.4/092—dc23
LC record available at https://lccn.loc.gov/2020027088
LC ebook record available at https://lccn.loc.gov/2020027089

ISBN: 978-0-367-51116-6 (hbk)
ISBN: 978-1-003-05247-0 (ebk)

Typeset in Times New Roman
by Apex CoVantage, LLC

# Contents

# Figures

# Introduction

There are literally thousands of books on leadership available on the market so does the world really need another one on the subject? This work builds upon those who have sought to challenge the underlying stereotypes and assumptions of leadership and further extends it by considering the salient question of how one might actually do leadership. In this regard, I believe this small book fulfills a role that is different from much of what has come before and this makes it worth reading.

The processes of leading are complex and when faced with such complexity a natural response might be to attempt to simplify the matter. However, as Alvesson (2002) has warned, in the process of saying everything about something, in effect nothing of value is actually said. The alternative is to acknowledge the complexity and deal with it. This book provides a structure for negotiating the way through such complexity.

Whilst I have not sought to present an extensive review of the leadership literature, I have used theory as the raw material to reflect upon in order to craft a more effective and accessible leadership. As will become clear, the body of theory is problematic and is unlikely to provide all the answers. It is nevertheless very helpful for stimulating reflexive interrogation about leadership across the organization and individual leadership in particular.

The book is organized into eight chapters that highlight some of the debates concerning the way leadership is understood and framed. These debates are grounded in a series of foundations that the book supports. Firstly, leadership should not be seen as being exclusively 'good'. I see leadership as being the behavior of all leaders, whether it be good, bad or indifferent. It is a mistake to credit leadership for delivering good outcomes when the bad outcomes are seen mostly as an absence of, or as a consequence of, behavior defined in the pejorative. Secondly, leadership is not a stable phenomenon. This means that leading in one context may be radically different in others; leaders may be very capable one day but less so on another. Thirdly, the practice of leading involves the complex interaction of a wide array of dynamics that need to be accommodated. Fourthly, our own moral compass informs the way leadership is practiced, but this too is rarely as fixed as believed. Our morals and values are less black and white but more strategically malleable as a consequence of the complex dilemmas to be faced.

The process of critically examining evidence and shaping one's practice through reflection locates leadership development as a learning process available to anyone prepared to make the trip. However, in doing so, one should be aware that the path might at times be discomforting. The book sets out a frame for making the individual the subject of inquiry, that is to say, to be objective about oneself through an iterative process of reflexive inquiry. This involves the leader paying attention to and examining the assumptions and central beliefs about oneself, leadership practice and the way one interacts with the world; using, thinking and questioning the varied forms of evidence that are available.

As part of this process I have posed some reflexive questions at the end of each chapter. It will prove valuable to address these questions, although the answers may not be immediately apparent. The questions are indicative of the type of interrogation that constitutes reflexive inquiry and I would suggest revisiting them whilst reading the book and beyond. It may prove to be a productive new habit to make a note of your responses and anything else that is of interest in some form of a journal and reflect upon these during the course of your journey.[1]

This book therefore is aimed as a guide to leaders of all types and experience that are faced with the challenge of leading. In essence, I agree that leadership is something vital to organizational functioning but argue against the consensus. I see leadership as something that is rather ordinary, common to all and grounded in the interactions between people functioning with good intent located within the parameters of their own contexts. In framing leadership this way, I open up the possibility that all those who seek to improve their own leadership practice can do so.

## Note

1 The use of a reflective journal is particularly useful in learning and development activities as it provides a good repository for thought and questions and maps progress over time. I heartily recommend Jenny Moon (2006) 'Learning Journals: A Handbook for Reflective practice and professional development' London: Routledge.

## References

Alvesson, M. (2002). *Understanding organizational culture*. London: Sage.

Moon, J. (2006). *Learning journals: A handbook for reflective practice and professional development*. London: Routledge.

# 1 What do we know about leadership?

Establishing the importance of leadership is often achieved through quoting some broad statistics such as those from the Society for Human Resource Management website, which asserts that $15.5bn is spent by US organizations on leadership development annually, and Amazon.com lists over 58,000 books with the word "leadership" in the title. As so much time and money are spent on leadership, a conclusion would be that leadership is important and that a lot must be known about it. However, there exist many questions within the field of leadership, meaning that there are equally as many questions about how to do leadership. This chapter starts by considering the various ways in which leadership has been defined, before suggesting that a plurality of definitions need not be a handicap. Following this, the assumptions about leadership that dominate the way leadership is thought about and supposed to be practiced is discussed, suggesting that a more grounded approach to leadership may prove to be more productive for the many.

## Defining leadership

It might appear odd to start an examination of leadership with an overt critique about the way leadership is understood and performed. I maintain that the way leadership is practiced is problematic, but rarely, if ever, is it presented in such a way. However, let me be clear – I do think leadership is important in organizations but perhaps not in the way it is traditionally presented. In a journal article, Gillespie (2016) asked the question, "Can management education create new model leaders?" and I think this really sits at the heart of the problem.

Gillespie asks a question concerning the absence of excellent leaders in society and bemoans the fact that whilst there are many very capable and competent managers, there exists a demonstrable lack of real leaders, defined as follows,

> someone with a vision that exists outside the norm; someone who can excite and marshal the untapped creative genius of people inside or outside of a formal organization; someone people stand in line to follow.
>
> Gillespie (2016, p. 53.)

The author is referring to the creative genius and large-scale vision of leaders and bemoans their absence without really thinking about, explaining or drawing attention to the alternative; if this kind of leadership is not apparent, perhaps it doesn't really exist in the manner suggested. The answer to this depends on how you think about leadership and the issues surrounding leadership – what is it exactly?

In the *Handbook of Leadership*, Ralph Stogdill (1974) makes the claim that there are as many definitions of leadership as there are people researching leadership. Whilst this claim was made with tongue in cheek, it is clear that there existed then and exist now many different and conflicting definitions of the same phenomenon. Surely this must create some kind of fundamental problem, but without knowing what it is, how does one actually do leadership? Drath (2001) suggests that leadership itself is not only a contested phenomenon but, like 'beauty,' it lies only in the eye of the beholder. Consequently, leadership is slippery 'beyond' definition, but one knows it when one sees it; does this effectively mean that anything can be considered leadership? Although it might not be clear what leadership is, it might be clearer what it isn't. As an example, one might suggest that leadership is not management, but even here the path is not clear, as Mintzberg (1973) asserts that leadership is a part of management. The practitioner may well suggest that a lack of clarity hinders progress in one's becoming a better leader, but we need to be mindful that, as focus is put on the issues, the complexities of leadership are addressed, and therefore understanding is enhanced in order to inform better practice.

Definitions make clear what is being talked about, but similarly, in the process of defining the subject, something may be omitted or reduced in significance. Definitions therefore matter, and so I offer the following provided by Alvesson, Blom and Sveningsson (2017) as I think it helps to have something to anchor the subject under discussion. I am not suggesting that this is the last word concerning leadership, but it will suffice for now.

> We therefore restrict leadership to be about people involved in an asymmetrical (unequal) relationship (formally or informally, permanently or temporarily, but not only momentarily) involving followers. Leaders

are interpersonally trying to define meaning/reality for others who are inclined to (on a largely voluntary basis) accept such meaning-making and reality-defining influencing acts.

Alvesson, Blom and Sveningsson (2017, p. 8)

This definition is interesting and useful for a number of reasons. Firstly, the authors have clearly restricted the scope for leadership; leadership can't be used to accommodate everything. This intentionally restricts those who, regardless of the issue, call for more leadership and present leadership as a panacea for all ills. Secondly, it acknowledges that there exists a relationship, though not necessarily between equals. Thirdly, the definition suggests that leaders are engaged in a process of meaning-making for others, and here understanding what's being stated is important. Both leaders and the led operate in a context that is defined by the organization, its culture, its sector, its markets and so on. It is important to note therefore that leadership is not enacted in a vacuum; it requires others and is in turn shaped by the dynamics that exist within that context. Helping others to understand and accept a specific context is what the authors are driving at here. Fourthly, and most critically, it is the mutually constructed meaning that forms the basis for all parties to agree on how to progress together.

The definition of leadership presented earlier excludes specific laws, rules, controls, outputs, behaviors and processes, values and/or competencies, and this is valuable for two reasons. Firstly, an effective and functioning organizational management has an essential role, too, and this definition does not seek to diminish its value. Additionally, the amount of time spent actually leading is relatively small compared to other tasks such as firefighting, administration, and, indeed, managing. Secondly, and most importantly, determining the required makeup of leadership practice when not sharing context is problematic; leadership can be practiced in many styles where no one style is better than others. It is less important that it is accepted as definitive but more that it grounds the understanding and actions for leadership practice. One of these grounded insights may be that more thought is given to how time is allocated when we are doing the tasks of our assigned role.

## Dealing with difference

Given the stated underlying framework for this book and our own leadership progress, it is necessary to develop a view on how to deal with conflicting theories. Here I am indebted to Wolff and Resnick (2012), as the intent of their book is to deal, objectively, with a number of grand economic theories that are seemingly at odds with one another. In doing so, they take some time to explain how one might deal with competing theories without suggesting that one is right, so the others therefore must clearly be wrong. There is something important to consider here, particularly in our contemporary world of increasing division, where it seems necessary to argue and justify the accuracy of our positions with others who seek to convince us of their own correctness.

It may be surprising, given the attention leadership receives within work and the media, that there is no unified view amongst scholars on the subject of how one should do leadership. Leadership therefore ought to be considered a pluralistic subject, comprising many voices that inevitably compete with and contradict one another. To engage with the material in order to show which view is right and which is wrong may well prove to be frustrating and ultimately pointless. As an alternative, I propose a more critical examination of the relevant merits and consider them not as competing for a monopoly on truth but more to view them as complementary knowledge of a particular subject, the utility of which is defined by our actions. The task is to consider each perspective and its respective merits, and in doing so, one needs to consider why another person holds a view that may be contradictory to our own. Since those who hold a view of the world are likely to act in a way that is in accord with their own view, they are likely to be in conflict with others who don't think and act in accord with that view. What we see is shaped in part by how we think just as much as how we think is shaped in part by what we see. Different theories not only explain the world differently, but they also influence us to see a world that requires a different explanation.

In the quest to understand a complex world, it is rather natural, but perhaps problematic, to seek simple solutions to inherently complex situations. One response to this, which is fairly typical within corporations, is to construct a list of skills and competences and then collectively structure and refer to them as the organization's leadership model or competency framework; however, the application of this model or framework is anything but straightforward. Ultimately, if an individual is to attain success within the organization, the model is required, to an extent, to be accepted and adhered to and evidence collected that demonstrates agreement with the model.

There are a number of problems with this approach, and to illustrate them I will borrow the framing used by Bones (2011) and Grint (1997). The first of these outlines the quest by the organization to identify critical skills and competences to end up with a list so extensive that in order to be able to deliver satisfactory leadership, the individual is required to become a Mary Poppins leader, "practically perfect in every way." I classify these as 'do everything well' models, and as a consequence, I am somewhat skeptical about the value of suggesting to the aspiring leader that all one need do is 'everything' and do it 'well,' simply because I don't see how any human who is a mix of relative strengths and weaknesses can legitimately do so.

The second framing sees the adherence to a defined and measurable model as akin to being strapped to the Procrustean 'iron bed.' Procrustes was a thief who invited travelers to stay the night. Subsequently, the guest was tied to an iron-framed bed where the host proceeded to stretch the guest's body to ensure a good fit for the bed; when parts of the individual's body extended beyond the bed frame, they were cut off. Can we ever be sure that the disposed parts are not those that comprise the essence of the person – the parts that made them a leader? The point here is that everyone fits the bed eventually (the model of leadership), but they are all dead. These two examples share an apparent similarity, and this creates a dilemma for our organizations; the individual is being asked to fit a prescribed model for which they are not designed. In doing so, the individual is likely to feel some discomfort ranging from the sense of being coerced into becoming something they aren't, or the process of fitting is unsuccessful, so progress is inhibited or stops. The problem here is that the framework sets out to contribute to the organization but in practice shapes people to be similar, despite the view that organizations need diversity through innovators, opportunists and entrepreneurs.

A further weakness in the way leadership is framed occurs as a consequence of attempts to make the model 'real' through the attainment of development goals and key performance indicators (KPIs) that demonstrate suitability for enhancement, and this comprises three related issues. Firstly, as success is a consequence of adherence to the model, it takes on a reality all its own. Critically this doesn't necessarily mean that the underlying model of leadership is the correct one; after all, given the view that leadership is context driven, at best the defined model might only be appropriate for a proportion of the time. This may be resolved by opening up the terms of the model or inserting competences, which are a response to uncertainty, such as 'Uses a flexible approach,' and this is the second issue. As our model expands to cover more and more terms or competences, how might we be sure which parts of it are actually valuable and meaningful?

The third issue takes certainty further. Frequently the success of an organizational venture is attributed to leadership, which further establishes leadership as essential to future successes. However, under what mechanism can these judgments be made with any degree of certainty when for the most part the judgments are made after the event or in essence are attributed to, and consequently may be limited in, causality. Just because someone claims something doesn't necessarily make it so. In making and believing in a claim of convenience, all of the other possible reasons are omitted, and acceptance must be given to the only surviving rationale.

## Assumptions about leadership

The problems of doing leadership within an organization are not limited to the frameworks that describe and structure leadership. At the heart of the problem are the assumptions about leadership that ultimately frame it in a particular way, as many of these assumptions and the associated attributes are questionable. The first assumption is the tendency to see leadership in only 'good' terms. I am well aware of perspectives that alternatively seek to problematize leadership, but whilst these are important, they are not representative of the way leadership is portrayed in the mainstream away from academic inquiry. Within this positive framing, leadership is good, the leaders themselves are demonstrably good, their actions are good and the outcomes of their leadership are also generally thought to be good. Nevertheless, approaching leadership in this way has inherent problems, as pointed out by Calás and Smircich (1991), where it is asserted that we can be seduced by the very notion of leadership, which as Grint (2010) suggests, leadership itself becomes 'sacred' and that assertions to the contrary are acts of profanity. In protecting the validity of good leadership, those in a leadership position who are incompetent or evil are given different titles so as not to impact the purity of the framing; Stalin was a tyrant, not a true leader.

With these warnings brought to the fore, the uncritical acceptance of leadership as good is stretching the point of credibility too much, and indeed our lived experiences tell us as much – there are many more examples of poor leadership within our work lives that suggest some attention should be given to them. As a consequence, therefore, I take the actions of leaders, be they good, bad or indifferent, to comprise the whole array of leadership behavior. Leadership may not only mean doing something that later turns out to be wrong, but may also involve doing something wrong for the right reasons. Clearly this is at odds with the dominant view, but at least this brings leadership down from its rarefied pedestal and grounds it into something more realistic and useful. After all, if it is acknowledged that there is much to be learned from studying inspiration, there is also considerable value in thinking about hubris. Where one might indicate what to do, the other warns of territories within which it is wise not to stray.

A second assumption relates to the apparent stability of leadership. Here it is assumed that good leaders have a currency regardless of the context and that good leaders demonstrate a marked evenness of approach. Such thinking tends to see leadership as something that is consistent and repeatable, and yet we know from our own experience that leaders may be successful in one particular context but not in another. This suggests that our own leadership currency may be high one day but may fall on another as a consequence of events that occur. But, if one were to consider all the possible variables that contribute to the way others perceive us that are attributable to our actions, how, against the odds, is our leadership ever to be perceived in a positive light?

In order to understand this more fully, Pfeffer (2015) points out that sometimes leaders are compelled to act in ways that are incongruous with most models of leadership. To illustrate the point, let's take one example. Good leaders are authentic, but which part of each of our complex makeup and identity is the authentic part? I am a middle-aged, male lecturer, employee, father, husband, son . . . which one of these constitutes the authentic me? Rarely therefore are individuals afforded the opportunity to be genuinely authentic, but in all likelihood, a different form of authenticity presents itself at different times. What this does is open up questions related to the dimensions of any framework deployed in order to define and frame leadership at work. Might honesty and integrity be in conflict with each other; might I prefer to be less than expressly honest if the situation demands it? This might lead to the conclusion that expectations of future actions are at best unrealistic and that what is really being talked about here is the extent to which leaders adhere to the expectations and how shortcomings are dealt with (or hidden) when they occur.

## The schools of leadership

Here consideration is given to the way in which leadership thinking has developed over time, as this has consequences not only for academia but also affects the way it is perceived and practiced within a wider constituency. To further this point, I refer to Rost (1991), a foundational text for anyone who is serious about researching and/or learning about leadership. As the book was written some time ago, it might be assumed that the main thrust of Rost's arguments have been resolved by progress in research. However, for the most part Rost's arguments are as pertinent today as they were when he wrote the book.

Rost outlines a number of deficiencies in the process and progress of leadership research generally. These can be loosely divided into two distinct areas. Firstly, Rost outlines issues with the way researchers have gone about studying leadership, and secondly, Rost addresses issues about the ways in which the findings of research have historically been presented. The first is rather technical and relates to issues of addressing social science, but it is not really appropriate to deal with them in much depth here. However, Rost considers the appropriateness of the methods used to uncover findings about leadership, suggesting that they are somewhat deficient. Others acknowledge this, most notably Bryman (1996) and Alvesson (1996), and leave a lasting impact upon the way leadership research has been conducted. The crux of the argument here is that studies of leadership have long been domi-nated by a particular method of researching that hasn't yielded much in the way of significant results, and as a consequence, the authors suggest using a wider array of methods.

More specifically, and at the heart of this concern, is that leadership thinking has been dominated by methods aligned to natural science, most commonly associated with management science and industrial psychology. As a response, many more recent studies have adopted methods more com-monly found in sociology or anthropology, but as some of these methods share many of the philosophical foundations, not much has changed as the results have remained as inconsistent and contradictory as before. Suffice it to say, what's being argued for is an approach that sees leadership in a more holistic way and takes shape by amalgamating varying approaches. This does not mean that there has been no substantial increase in understand-ing and developments made in complexity science and leadership,[1] and the leader-member exchange theory (LMX)[2] illustrates this point admirably.

The second substantive part of Rost's critique refers to the way leader-ship research is often presented. Should one read a chronological review of the leadership literature, it would be noted that the trajectory of the litera-ture falls into some rather convenient stages, beginning with trait analysis, and moving on to behavioral, through to contingent or situational leader-ship, to arrive in the early1980s with a group of theories that were at the time classified by Alan Bryman as comprising the New Leadership school to subsequently be classified as neo-charismatic theories, and then finally as a collection of perspectives that generally have no specific grouping but may be seen as leadership theories of late modernity. The problem with this, according to Rost, is that the classification is just too tidy and too convenient. When outlined chronologically, the assumption may well be that a growth in the understanding of leadership has occurred to arrive in the modern day with understanding at its zenith. The idea here is that the-ory develops as a consequence of some weakness or deficiency which is replaced by something with greater explanatory power. So according to the aforementioned history, trait theories are replaced with behavioral theories, which in turn are overwritten by situational theories, which are displaced by neo-charismatic theories and so on. The core of the problem, however, is that these previous theories didn't disappear but were reinvented in contem-porary research to the extent that the theories of late modernity comprise theories from the whole history of leadership thinking. As an example, trait theories paved the way for the consideration and allocation of leadership ability to the 'great men' of yesteryear. However, there is still a fascination with the great men of contemporary society and with business and politics more particularly. So just as the leadership of William Lever, JP Morgan and John D Rockefeller, amongst others, was celebrated at the turn of the 20th century, so today is the leadership of Richard Branson, Elon Musk and Jamie Dimon.

Leadership is an integral part of organizational functioning, but when approached in a misguided way, it can be obstructive to the group and dispiriting to the individual who has in essence set themselves up to fail. In order for leadership to retain its validity, we need to displace the grandiosity of leadership thinking and replace it with something more grounded and faithful, something practicable, grounded in our own reflexive thinking.

## Reflexive questions

Refer back to the statement from Gillespie – does this statement resonate with you? Do you agree or disagree with the writer?

How is leadership presented in your organization and what implications does this have for the way leadership is both practiced and measured?

## Notes

1 Uhl Bien, M., Marion, R. and McKelvey, B. (2007). Complexity leadership theory: Shifting leadership from the industrial to the knowledge era. *Leadership Quarterly*, 18(4), pp. 298–318.
2 Martin, R., Epitropaki, O., Thomas, G. and Topakas, A. (2010). A critical review of Leader-Member Relationship (LMX) research: Future prospects and directions. *International Review of Industrial and Organizational Psychology*, 25, pp. 61–91.

## References

Alvesson, M. (1996). Leadership studies: From procedure and abstraction to reflexivity and situation. *The Leadership Quarterly*, 7(4), pp. 455–485.

Alvesson, M., Blom, M. and Sveningsson, S. (2017). *Reflexive leadership: Organising in an imperfect world*. London: Sage.

Bryman, A. (1996). Leadership in organizations. In: S.R. Clegg, C. Hardy, and W.R. Nord, eds., *Handbook of organization studies*. London: Sage, pp. 276–292.

Bones, C. (2011). *The cult of the leader: A manifesto for more authentic business*. Chichester: John Wiley & Sons.

Calas, M.B. and Smirchich, L. (1991). Voicing seduction to silence leadership. *Organization Studies*, 12(4), pp. 567–602.

Drath, W. (2001). *The deep blue sea: Rethinking the source of leadership*. San Francisco: Jossey Bass.

Gillespie, J. (2016). Can management education create new model leaders. *Management Teaching Review*, 1(1), pp. 52–57.

Grint, K. (1997). *Leadership: Classical, contemporary and critical approaches.* Oxford: Oxford University Press.

Grint, K. (2010). The sacred in leadership: Separation, sacrifice and silence. *Organization Studies*, 31(1), pp. 89–107.

Mintzberg, H. (1973). *The nature of managerial work.* New York: Harper & Row.

Pfeffer, J. (2015). *Leadership BS: Fixing workplaces and careers one truth at a time.* New York: Harper Collins.

Rosenweig, P. (2007). *The halo effect.* London: Simon and Schuster.

Rost, J. (1991). *Leadership for the 21st century.* Westport, CT: Praeger.

Stogdill, R.M. (1974). *Handbook of leadership: A survey of theory and research.* New York: Free Press.

Wolff, R. and Resnick, S. (2012). *Contending economic theories: Neoclassical, Keynesian and Marxian.* Cambridge: MIT Press.

# 2 Mainstream theories, visions and transformations

In this chapter, I will briefly cover the main perspectives of leadership starting with the great man theories developed in the 19th century up to the dominant theories of today. Particular attention will be given to the theories of the New Leadership school, as these have had a powerful influence on the way leadership in our organizations and society more generally is viewed. In essence, these theories are normative; they have framed expectations about what leaders should do and how they ought to behave. A principal observation to be made here is that the leader is at the center of the theory, and as such, these theories may be described as leader-centric. More recently researchers have broadened their perspective to incorporate a wider array of factors in leadership theorizing, nevertheless there still exists a strong tendency to look at the most senior leaders and to draw conclusions from this population.

## Are leaders born or made?

The view of individuals who are born to lead is embraced in some of the earliest forms of leadership thinking when in the mid-19th century Thomas Carlisle wrote about great men achieving great things at a time when the British Empire was dominant. It is clearly inferred here that leadership ability is linked directly to a genetic trait or attribute given at birth. Despite clear evidence of the existence of notable leaders who are not men, such as Emeline Pankhurst, Florence Nightingale and Elizabeth Garret Anderson, to name a few, it is obvious that we are referring to males born to families of privilege, as they would be most likely to hold positions of authority and provided with the opportunity to lead. Men of privilege dominate theories of the time, and as such, the theory also may be seen to be a product of their time. Consider the terms used to describe contemporary leadership and then reflect upon the practice of the 'great man theory' leaders of yesteryear.

How much time do you think the Victorian leaders of the empire might have given to considering emotional intelligence or fairness with respect to equality and/or diversity?

Whilst the nature part of the debate asserts that leaders are born with the skills and attributes for leadership at birth, the opposing side suggests that leaders can be made, in that traits and behaviors can be taught and learned. Whilst the first perspective suggests that leaders comprise a small and special part of the population, this second perspective implies that anyone can become a leader of great effectiveness. This perspective corresponds to those commonly referred to as trait and style (behavioral) perspectives of leadership. The earlier trait school of thinking, which was prevalent in the 1930–1950s, aimed to identify a series of attributes and skills that, once identified, could determine a framework for predicting leadership success. This approach, however, was considered somewhat simplistic, and as a consequence, the style perspective became more dominant in the late 1940s when large-scale research programs conducted by Ohio State University attempted to determine successful leadership styles. Where trait thinking may be seen to correspond to the selection of leaders, the style approach more accurately relates to the training of leaders as the assumption here is clearly that leadership ability is something that can be learned. As with the earlier description of 'great man' thinking, the leadership theories of the 1930–1960s can also be seen as a product of their time. The shift to skills to be learned corresponds to the development of the Tavistock Institute[1] in the UK and a wider, more general, appreciation of human behavior and the human relations' perspectives of organizational functioning and development.

In any particular group, there tends to be very enthusiastic advocates for both sides of this debate. Perhaps it may prove more useful if we stop thinking of polar opposites and consider a continuum as this more closely represents our own experiences. Contact is made with individuals known to possess skills and attributes that are different from others'. Some people have genetic gifts that make them more predisposed to becoming better athletes or musicians, amongst other professions. This observation doesn't remove the possibility that anyone can develop his or her abilities as an athlete or a musician, however. It may not be possible to attain the same levels of proficiency as those with more genetic gifts, but certainly improvements can be made. An individual may well be born with certain skills and attributes pertinent to leadership, but it is highly unlikely that someone is born without any of the requisite abilities to lead.

Some people may fail at being a leader when measured by a particular framework, but perhaps it is the framework and/or the measurement that's at fault. Does the observation that the skills and abilities held by an individual have no particular resonance with a specific leadership framework suggest that they have no leadership capacity when they clearly have skills and attributes that have some other value. I would strongly argue that this is not a solid foundation from which to build either individual or organizational leadership capability or identify leadership potential. Consequently, therefore, leaders can be both born and made, both the nature and nurture element of leadership development has currency as one side (nature) provides the raw materials and building blocks from which to learn and develop (nurture). What is needed is a full consideration of the view that leadership can be practiced in many different ways and styles.

## The New Leadership school

By the late 1970s, leadership scholarship was experiencing a general air of malaise. A subsequent shot in the arm was provided by a group of theories that signaled a new way of conceptualizing and researching leadership; collectively these theories were referred to as the school of New Leadership (Bryman, 1986). The various theories depict a conception of the leader as someone capable of defining organizational reality through an articulation of a vision, which is a reflection of how he or she defines the mission of the organization and the values that underpin it. Although these theories may be seen as a repackaging of existing theory, collectively the New Leadership school has developed a resonance amongst scholars and practitioners alike, which has meant that its theoretical underpinnings have come to represent the generally accepted view of leadership, particularly as far as our organizations are concerned.

During the 1980s, leadership researchers became very interested in the revitalization and specific transformation of mainly US companies as a consequence of increasing competition from the developing world and specifically Japan. The New Leadership approach seemed to tie in to an increasing appetite for stories about heroic chief executives and a growing awareness of organizations and their visions. Additionally, it may be that stories of individual celebrities from business and other walks of life appeal to our own culture; there is a strong resonance for the heroic business leader in societies and cultures that may be determined to be more individualistic, and particularly those with a strong Anglo-Saxon tradition. Like other theories already addressed, perhaps consideration should be given to the view that New Leadership theories correspond with a period of corporate challenge requiring that a hero stand up and lead, and they can also be appreciated as a product of their time.

Yukl (1989) suggests that it is the interplay between transformational and charismatic processes that provides the foundations for the standards for effective leadership and establishes the essential foundations of the

New Leadership approach. Both transformational and charismatic theories of leadership, whilst based on earlier theories, are broader in scope and as such represent an important step in the development of the leadership literature. The theories of the New Leadership school have come to comprise the dominant framework of leadership as practiced and advocated in contemporary business, and consequently one may well recognize elements of them in frameworks of the workplace. Nevertheless, there remains plenty of scope for these theories to be challenged, as regardless of how frequently they are espoused, they do not corner the market on truth. Although this book does not set out to comprehensively outline perspectives of leadership, the New Leadership school has proven to be particularly influential, so a brief outline of some of the theories is given next.

## House's charismatic leadership theory (1977)

This theory specifies indicators of charismatic leadership that involve the attitudes and perceptions of followers about the leader. The theory also deals with leader traits that increase the likelihood of being perceived as charismatic, including a strong need for power, high self-confidence and assured beliefs. Behaviors of charismatic leaders include impression management, articulation of an appealing vision, communication of high expectations and expressions of confidence in follower ability. In addition, charismatic leaders set examples for followers through their own behavior and can act to arouse follower motives appropriate to the task.

Bernard Bass noted some conceptual limitations to the theory and recommended extending it to include additional traits, behaviors, indicators of charisma and facilitating conditions. He proposed that charismatic leaders were more likely to appear in crises where formal authorities have failed and traditional values and methods have fallen under scrutiny.

## Conger and Kanungo's charismatic theory (1987)

The version of charismatic theory proposed by Conger and Kanungo (1987) is based on the assumption that charisma is an attributed phenomenon. Followers attribute charismatic qualities to a leader based on their observations of the leader's behavior and the outcomes associated with it. Such behaviors are not assumed to be present in every charismatic leader to the same extent, and the relative importance of each behavior can vary, dependent upon the situation. The behaviors include the following: enthusiastic advocacy of a compelling vision differentiated from the status quo and yet still within follower tolerance, making self-sacrifices and risking personal loss in the perusal of the vision and undertaking unconventional actions in order to achieve the vision. Traits enhancing the attribution of charisma include self-confidence, impression management skills, high cognitive ability and social empathy required to understand the needs and values of followers.

Attributed charisma is more likely to be found in a leader who relies on expert and referent power to influence followers, as opposed to authority and participation. Charismatic leaders are likely to emerge when there is a crisis requiring major change or followers are dissatisfied with the status quo. However, in the absence of a genuine crisis, a leader may be able to create dissatisfaction in order to demonstrate expertise in dealing with the problem in unconventional ways.

## Burns's theory of transforming leadership (1978)

The theory of "transforming leadership" was developed from skilled observation of a number of political leaders. Burns (1978) described leadership as a process of evolving interrelationships in which leaders influence followers and are influenced in turn to modify their behavior as their followers respond or resist. Transforming leadership is viewed as a micro-level influence process between individuals and a macrolevel process of mobilizing power to change structures and institutions. According to Burns, leaders seek to increase followers' consciousness by appealing to their higher ideals and values and not their baser instincts. Followers are thus elevated from their everyday selves to their better selves. Transforming leadership can be exhibited by anyone in an organization regardless of their position as it may involve the influencing of peers or superiors as well as subordinates.

Burns contrasts transforming leadership with transactional leadership, in which followers are motivated primarily by appeals to their own self-interest. He also differentiates transforming leadership from the transacting element, which is influence based on bureaucratic authority, which emphasizes power, rules and traditions.

## Bass's theory of transformational/transactional leadership (1985)

Bass's approach draws heavily on the work of Burns but goes much further in two respects (Bass and Avolio, 1990; Bass, 1985). Firstly, as opposed to the opposite ends of a continuum, Bass sees transformational and transactional leadership as separate dimensions. The ideal approach is to demonstrate elements of both forms of leadership. Secondly, in contrast to Burns's generalized style of discussing the two types of leadership, Bass has specified the individual components and developed a series of indicators for each component.

Transformational leadership refers to those processes that influence major changes in the attitudes and assumptions of organizational members and the building of commitment for the organization's vision/mission, objectives and strategies, recognized by the outputs of the transformed organization. Transformational leadership involves influence by a leader on subordinates, resulting in the empowerment of subordinates to influence the transformation of the organization. Transformational leadership is therefore seen as a shared process, involving the actions of leaders throughout the organization and not just those actions of the foremost hierarchical leader.

In later theorizing, the full range leadership theory (FRLT) was conceived. A distinction can be made between four aspects of transformational leadership: namely, idealized influence (formerly charisma), inspirational motivation, intellectual stimulation and individualized consideration. Three aspects of transactional leadership are added to the model: specifically, contingent reward, active management-by-exception and passive management-by-exception. In the major variation away from earlier models is the inclusion of a behavior type for when leaders choose to abstain from influencing subordinates. This is referred to as laissez-faire leadership. The model is summarized in Figure 2.1. Research findings on the model have shown charisma and inspiration to be the two components of leader behavior that are most strongly associated with outcomes such as the performance of subordinates. The transformational elements (the top four boxes) interact to influence changes in followers, and these combined effects are what differentiate this approach from that of charismatic leadership. Transformational leaders seek to inspire and elevate subordinates; with charismatic leaders, the opposite sometimes may occur.

It has been suggested that the aforementioned theories are similar as they share the same antecedents; it would be more appropriate therefore to consider them all as a neo-charismatic group of theories (Beyer, 1999). As the name implies, it is the dimension of charisma and/or inspiration that runs through the models. If one were to look at job adverts for senior managers that appear on influential recruitment sites and in newspapers, clear evidence can be found to illustrate the depth to which inspiration has entered contemporary discourse on the one hand and the perceived importance of inspiration as an essential part of leadership on the other. The question remains therefore whether in practice inspiration and charisma are the same thing or to what extent they are similar. One aspect that might suggest that they are at least linked is the view that as theory developed and coincided with evidence to support a negative view of charisma (see Chapter 7), the word was displaced by other words such as 'inspiring' and 'motivation'

**Idealized Influence (charisma)**: Envisioning a valued future, articulating how to reach it. Sets high standards and uses self as an example that followers identify with and wish to follow.

**Inspirational Motivation:** The leader provides simplified and symbolic appeals in support of a goal.

**Intellectual Stimulation:** Encouraging followers to address old problems to be more creative and innovative.

**Individualized Consideration:** Treating each follower individually with different needs for development and support.

**Contingent Reward:** Reward or promise of reward provided in exchange for meeting standards.

**Management by Exception:** Active or Passive. Corrective action in light of failure to meet standards (correction, feedback, reproof, sanctions and disciplinary action).

**Laissez Faire:** Unconcerned, procrastination and avoidance of issues and decisions.

*Figure 2.1* The full range leadership theory. Author's own, informed by Avolio, Bass and Jung (1999).

whilst additionally providing a role model to follow. If one considers the problems of how to be charismatic or how one can inspire and motivate others, an interesting parallel with the nature-nurture debate becomes apparent. Charisma as generally understood is an innate trait something the individual leader possesses and therefore corresponds to the nature element of the debate. Inspiration and motivation however might more closely be associated with the nurture position as this is something that is more closely aligned with leadership Behavior.

The notion of charisma itself is drawn from the works of Max Weber, who was at his most prominent during the epoch of the great man theory. His work problematizes and draws attention to the reasons why some individuals gain a position of authority that is unexplained by recourse to other forms of authority, traditional authority sanctioned by norms and heritage and legal/rational authority as a consequence of a belief and competence in formal and rational forms of law. Weber suggests that charismatic authority is based upon an extraordinary appeal. The etymology of the word 'charisma' is from the Greek and translated means "Gift from God (or the gods)"; charisma therefore is something that is bestowed upon the individual as a gift or through divine intervention at birth. Whilst not underplaying the importance of charisma, the concept in this Weberian understanding, when transferred to contemporary neo-charismatic theory, refers to something otherworldly and difficult to grasp. The question remains here as to whether the construct of charisma is a convenient method through which we can explain the unexplainable.

The idea of charismatic leadership asserts that in order to be effective, the majority, the led, are prepared to invest so much in the authority of the gifts bestowed upon the charismatic hero. If charisma was a possession, then the individual charismatic and their charisma would always shine through. Empirically this just isn't the case. There appears to be no such thing as a universal charismatic; just as Blair was fêted during his successful administration, this waned as a consequence of the Iraqi conflict and his period outside of 10 Downing Street. Lee Iacocca, once known as the savior of Chrysler Motors, also took the company into a depressing tailspin very soon after the books and papers had finished telling his success story. This isn't conclusive proof that these individuals are not charismatic or that charismatics do not exist. I don't discount their existence as it may well be that supremely talented and charismatic individuals do exist and rise to authority, but the counter to this must be considered: they are extraordinarily rare. Similarly, this doesn't suggest that charisma is not a feature of leadership, but more that if it exists in its theorized form, then consideration must be given to the fact that charisma, like leadership itself, is less definitive and robust.

A more contemporary development of the neo-charismatic viewpoint can be found in the importance given to inspiration and motivation. Whilst there may be little doubt as to their stated importance, the question remains as to how one should inspire and motivate others. There is a strong reliance on the efficacy of leadership visions that elevates commitment and motivation to the vision and brings it into reality. Peters and Waterman's (1982) work is one of the formative publications that supports the importance of a vision to corporate success. The book was hugely popular as a consequence of the compelling case studies contained within. The problem is that, despite their visions, all of the companies depicted struggled in subsequent years, indicating at least that a vision might not be the catchall solution to the problems of motivation and long-term success. There are a number of reasons to question the potency of leaders and their visions.

In the first instance, some work is just not very visionary. A claim that the organization is engaged in changing or leading the world may not really carry much weight, particularly if the business or organization itself is doing something foundational or mainstream. There may well be cases of business that are extraordinary, but for the most part, despite their relative importance, they just aren't for the bulk of the people who work inside the organization. As the majority of the workforce is unlikely to share the contexts of the senior leaders and vice versa, it would need to be a very compelling vision to motivate them. There is a story accredited to John F Kennedy, who, upon asking the janitor what he did at NASA, received the reply that he was "putting a man on the moon." Seventeenth-century architect, Sir Christopher Wren, asked the exact same question to stonemasons, and one replied that he was "helping build a beautiful cathedral." These apocryphal stories prove the point, but how common are stories like these, and why aren't our organizations full of them, relative to all those employed?

Perhaps it is worth considering that by focusing on the transformational parts of leadership issues, the transactional elements tend to be neglected, and yet it is here that the leader communicates directly and personally with the subordinate worker in order to spell out the consequences for doing (or not doing) a particular task. Economic theory suggests that people work to maximize their own utility through self-interest, indicating a relationship between what someone does and how they are rewarded. Just as it's unlikely that people are solely motivated by a vision, it is just as unlikely that people are solely motivated by some perceived reward. A worker earning minimum wage is unlikely to work harder if the only reward is an increase in the firm's share price, for example. A story that depicts the future wellbeing of a company and the benefits to all of its workforce expressed in terms that have meaning for the individual would demonstrate more clearly how and why someone should give a bit more toward the organization's goal.

The impact of the visions of transformational leaders is also likely to be short lived. It is entirely possible that someone is enthused and motivated by speeches, presentations and publications related to the organization's future and by the commitments and sacrifices of the organization's leaders, but how long does this euphoric state really exist relative to the total time spent at work? One may leave the auditorium or meeting full of expectation and enthusiasm and have it all dashed by the realities of work as made tangibly real by the emails that have arrived in the intervening period. It is worth considering the view that reliance upon the explicit rhetoric of transformational leadership may have a limited currency and that the practice of leadership as epitomized by a grandiose framing of narrative and gesture ought to be displaced by something more grounded and meaningful.

## The contemporary dominant perspective

Models of the neo-charismatic perspective dominate the contemporary organizational landscape and have become theories that define our expectations and assumptions about the way leadership should work. They are *normative* theories and may also be referred to as *functional* theories. Functionalism is drawn from a body of work produced in the late 19th century, where it is maintained that the institutions, roles and norms that comprise society are integral and important to the long-term survival and health (functioning) of that society. Functionalist theories dominate not just leadership thinking but management and business studies more generally, and here the phenomenon under observation within a given society contributes functionally to it, and the phenomenon of leadership contributes to society in ways that can be observed and determined. Leadership thinking, as outlined earlier, may be considered to be both functionalist and normative.

According to Burrell and Morgan (1979), there exists the possibility of seeing the world in different ways, and consequently, they provide four specific lenses for looking at human phenomena. The essential proposition here is that all theories about organizations (and by extension, work, business and all associated phenomenon including leadership) can be derived from the way in which theories of science and of society are perceived. One approach may be favored over another because it conforms to a set of explicit or implicit assumptions that are held about the way the world works; in other words, people adopt the view that is most comfortable to them. Explicitly stepping outside of the comfort zone and considering other approaches by viewing the world through a different lens may provide insights that were previously hidden.[2] It is this critical interrogation of assumptions about how the world works that forms the core reflexivity processes for leadership development, which are unpacked in Chapter 8. Studying, defining and acting on what constitutes leadership is potentially limited only by how we think, talk and write about it. The findings of normative-functionalist theories presented as objective truth very quickly close down alternatives that may fundamentally change how we see and do leadership, and under such restrictions perhaps consideration ought to be given to the notion that we get the leaders we deserve.

## Reflexive questions

How do your ideological orientations influence your understanding of leadership; for example, are you caught up in certain ideals – visionary, strategic, coaching – that are potentially seductive? Do these beliefs constrain your ability to understand alternative frames of leadership?

From where might your assumptions about leadership originate?

## Notes

1 The Tavistock Institute of Human Relations (founded in 1947) emerged from the social department of Tavistock Clinic (founded in 1920) and has a remarkable history between research into organizational behavior and organizations as systems. This work was to become synonymous with the human relations school of organizational thinking. For further information I recommend the article on the British Library's website about the Tavistock Institute found at www.bl.uk/business-and-management/editorials/tavistock-institute-of-human-relations.

A separate body was also formed from members of the Tavistock Clinic and the Directorate of Army Psychiatry to become the Tavistock Institute of Human Behavior (1946).

2 Burrell and Morgan (1979) set out four specific paradigms, a short outline of which is given here.

The Functionalist paradigm

This is identified as the dominant paradigm for organizational research. It tends to be highly pragmatic, problem oriented and committed to a philosophy of social engineering as a basis for social change through consent. Observations are presented as facts, which provide a basis for conclusions as a step toward gaining a better understanding and toward improving society in general.

The Radical Humanist paradigm

Here understanding of social order is seen as a product of coercion, rather than as consent, and supports the view of society overthrowing or transcending the limitations of existing social arrangements. It can be appreciated as a brand of social theorizing designed to provide a critique of the status quo. The radical humanist paradigm in essence is based upon an inversion of the basis of the functionalist paradigm. The potential for change is as a consequence of ideas that liberate individuals from a form of mental prison. Life experiences are subject to critical reflection and as such can inspire opposition to forces of control.

The Interpretive Paradigm

In essence, developed as a critique of overt functionalism, the main concern here is to understand how society is socially constructed (see Chapter 4), and by association, therefore, it perceives society as subjective-interpretive. The world as we understand it derives from a consequence of meanings and understandings developed and transferred through differing social agents. Consequently, we are part of what we know. The objective analysis of the world is therefore an impossibility.

The Radical Structuralist Paradigm

Developed out of Marxist and Weberian analyses of social life this paradigm is concerned with modes of control embedded within society and the ways through which these can be overturned. Here the view is that change is possible through a focus on the controlling structures of social life. This perspective is particularly difficult to comprehend without a deeper understanding of associated perspectives and is also mercifully rare in organizational thinking, and so I think it is safe to acknowledge it but to swiftly move on.

# References

Alvesson, M., Blom, M. and Sveningsson, S. (2017). *Reflexive leadership: Organising in an imperfect world.* London: Sage.

Avolio, B.J., Bass, B.M. and Jung, D.I. (1999). Re-examining the components of transformational and transactional leadership using the multifactor leadership questionnaire. *Journal of Occupational and Organizational Psychology,* 72, pp. 441–462.

Bass, B.M. (1985). *Leadership and performance beyond expectations.* New York: Free Press.

Bass, B.M. (1998). *Transformational leadership: Industrial, military, and educational impact.* Mahwah, NJ: Lawrence Erlbaum.

Bass, B.M. and Avolio, B. (1990). *Transformational leadership development: Manual for the multifactor leadership questionnaire.* Palo Alto, CA: Consulting Psychologists Press.

Beyer, J. (1999). Taming and promoting charisma to change organizations. *The Leadership Quarterly,* 10(2), pp. 307–330.

Bryman, A. (1986). *Leadership in organizations.* London: Keegan Paul.

Burns, J.M. (1978). *Leadership.* New York: Harper & Row.

Burrell, G. and Morgan, G. (1979). *Sociological paradigms and organizational analysis.* London: Heinemann Press.

Conger, J.A. and Kanungo, R.A. (1987). Toward a behavioral theory of charismatic leadership in organizational settings. *Academy of Management Review,* 12, pp. 637–647.

Yukl, G. (1989). Managerial leadership: A review of theory and research. *Journal of Management,* 15(2), pp. 251–289.

# 3 Leadership, organization and teams

It can be demonstrated that perceptions of leadership shift to meet its context, and so I see leadership as shifting to meet the current environment. One of most notable changes is the increasing reliance on the use and deployment of teams as the primary vehicle for responding to complex working contexts. Correspondingly, there is an increase in trying to understand how to lead a team more effectively. The literature on team leadership is relatively new but is mostly framed on models of the past. Newer, more radical, perspectives distanced from functional antecedents such as networked, systemic and distributed approaches may offer new and profound ways of leading, the implications of which are discussed in this chapter.

## What is a team?

It is difficult pinpoint exactly when the interest in team-based leadership first came to prominence. Early psychologists from a psychoanalytical tradition theorized about the interplay between relationships from at least the turn of the 20th century. In more contemporary times, there is a much more explicit focus on the leadership of teams, and research in this area over the last decade has grown substantially. In its earlier days, team leadership researchers took individualistic and organizational-level theories of leadership and applied them to the team, but the results of this particular path of inquiry were generally less than conclusive; as an example, situational theorist, Fieldler (1967), cited the team as one of the variables to be considered when plotting an effective approach to leading. In other words, the adaption and application of existing theories were not fruitful, and this required that team leadership establish its own particular approach. It is notable that both practitioners in the field and researchers have stated that very little is known about how leaders create and lead teams.

It may well be that confusion exists in establishing exactly what comprises a team. Classifications such as 'team,' 'group' and 'pseudo team' are used commonly but are less than clear. Consequently, we ought to agree on a definition that helps us understand the differences between the various groupings. Teams therefore are defined as: groups of people working together in an organization who are recognized as a team, who agree on team-level objectives and work closely together to achieve those objectives, who are clear about the objectives and have the autonomy to decide how to undertake a task and who communicate regularly to regulate team processes. Similar groupings that do not demonstrate some or all of the criteria mentioned here still may be considered teams by the organization and are defined as 'pseudo teams' by researchers in this area. A group remains a group until it becomes a team, or at least until the group acknowledges itself as being a team.

Within the different kinds of teams, there is an enormous array of dynamics that makes each team different: size, diversity, demographics, personalities, cognitive abilities, social abilities, socialization and development, processes of decision-making, processes of effectiveness and so on. Teams and team functioning therefore are perhaps more complex than assumed. It seems strange therefore that the team would be chosen as the primary work unit charged with delivering complex organizational objectives in response to unprecedented levels of complexity. It might be assumed from this that, where teams are employed, the results are sufficient to continue to place emphasis on the effectiveness of the team unit. This may well run contrary to our own experiences, where most of us have in all likelihood been involved in teamwork that has ranged from, at best, suboptimal, to at worst, an unmitigated disaster. However, can an explanation for this discrepancy be that reliance upon teamwork means that we more readily attribute success to the team, thereby 'proving' the effectiveness of working on a team?

If research is to be relied upon to inform our view and practice of team leadership, then by necessity, we have to be content with the research that deals with the most prevalent kind of team, the co-located team, in which all of the constituent members of the team share a similar geographical location and are in close proximity to each other; distance does not cause an obstacle to team functioning. Leadership of co-located teams tends to be examined through the lens of functional effectiveness. That is to say, leadership is viewed as social problem-solving; the more that leadership puts into the team, the greater the amount of designated outputs as the leader resolves the problems associated with team production. In practice, the job of the leader is to do whatever is required for the team to deliver its outcomes. This may also include consideration of those tasks that are not explicitly considered by the team unit.

Specifically, such a leadership approach has three closely linked elements. The first is that leadership is seen as fulfilling the role of providing meaning. Leaders link the team to their context by defining the events that occur within that context. The leader explains what's going on and why and relates the team's tasks to those events. Secondly, the leadership function is required because it is assumed that problems will arise that require the leader's input to resolve them. This does not mean that the actual problem resolution cannot come from someone within the team who is not the designated leader. And third, functional leadership is not defined by a prescribed set of behaviors, as these are determined by assisting the team in problem-solving. In summary, the leader contributes to team problem-solving processes through the search and structuring of information to use in solving problems, managing personnel resources and managing material resources.

Research has demonstrated that the two areas that receive the most attention from leaders are, firstly, structuring the team and task, and secondly, establishing the purpose of the team itself. The role of the leader on the team here has shifted from functional problem-solving to one of developing the team to solve its own problems by dispersing leadership throughout the team. In the early stages, the focus is on establishing goals that build social and task capabilities. Following this early phase and moving into the action phase, the focus shifts to maintaining team coherence. This is principally due to the fact that during the action phase, it has been noticed that agreement and conformity decline, possibly as a consequence of individuals prioritizing certain aspects of the task over others. Toward the end of the action phase, as the task itself nears completion, the leader again shifts focus to concentrate on reflection to facilitate learning, in a sense, aiding team members to be better team members in the future. With respect to team development, the leader is engaged in the process of moving members along a development continuum ranging from novice to expert.

The models of leadership employed here appear to be redolent of models from the school of situational (or contingency) leadership that were prevalent in the1960s, maintaining a focus on the task and the led. It is stated that the leader should be capable of not only processing all of the variable data before plotting the most appropriate course of action but also has a framework within which to determine what skills the future teams are likely to need. If the business world is changing as fast as is claimed, then perhaps skills learned in one time and place may become a hindrance in another; in effect the leader cannot know.

Just as situational/contingency leadership ultimately was displaced because of its sheer complexity and lack of explanatory capacity, there is a very real sense of déjà vu here with respect to team leadership. In attempts to simplify teamwork to a manageable extent, there are important dynamics that have been left out of the equation. These tend to be those that don't sit comfortably within team leadership but are very real to leaders and those being led. Firstly, attention needs to be given to the politics of the situation and the external political influences associated with members of the team as a consequence of their own histories and influences. Secondly, the concept of power is underemployed in the team situation. Leaders have power, and the led have less; displays of power by leaders are likely to be labeled as 'autocratic,' 'authoritative' or 'bullying,' amongst other phrases, anything but 'leadership.' Finally, team members may well engage in resistance, even if it is the resistance of micro-politics. There is a well-observed phenomenon that has been referred to as 'social loafing,' where the individual deliberately fails to fully engage with either the task or the team members but prefers to sit back and allow the other members of the team to do the work, using the team environment to coast and relax.

According to the Sage Handbook of Leadership referring to team leadership,

> For example leaders impact cognition by instilling an understanding of the mission and each persons contribution to performance, Leaders impact motivational processes directly by motivational strategies that are practiced and indirectly through their planning, coordination, personnel development and feedback behaviours . . . leaders manage the climate of the team in order to control conflict and team norms. Finally leaders influence team coordination by developing the teams awareness of what resources are available to the team, offering clear task strategies, monitoring environmental changes and providing developmental and goal oriented feedback to the team.
>
> Burke (2014, p. 339)

I'm not sure how much help this is to those given the responsibility of leading a team, as it seems very similar to much of the dominant thinking on leadership in that the leader is some kind of super human equipped with the skills to do 'everything well' in support of the 'all is good' conceptualizations of leadership. Models such as this, unconsciously at least, clearly establish such an exalted standard and an expectation of standards so that the probability of the leader failing to attain the expected standard is really, and possibly unfairly, quite high. In order to unpack and understand this a little more completely, a consideration of some of the foundational work from Sigmund Freud on the psychology of groups ought to be made.

Freud watched and analyzed crowds in order to hypothesize about what was going on. He observed that at times of crisis, a leader would emerge from within the group. Importantly, the leader is a member of the group, one of a general population, with no more natural capacity or capability than the group contains within itself. It is the group itself that bestows the extraordinary abilities on the leader and has a commensurate level of expectations about the leader. Freud would claim that this is because of the group's strong desire for the prototypical father figure to emerge, protect and keep the group safe. The leader is someone who is a container for the anxiety felt by the group caused by the external threat and who makes the group feel secure. However, it is possible that the newly appointed father figure will fail to meet expectations, and just as the group raised them up as its leader, the group can and will depose them. After the event, the individual is scrutinized and exposed as being no more exceptional than the rest; however, this doesn't stop the process from occurring again and again as the next leader is charged with providing security and safety.

This outline might appear rather ill-founded or specious as it runs contrary to much of the established thinking regarding heroic leaders and their capacity to resolve difficult situations. However, examples like this are common. Perhaps someone has been promoted (or more likely parachuted in from outside), after a period of exceptional performance, to a leadership position elsewhere, and after a period of time in their new role, they fail to meet expectations and may move on as a perceived failure.

### New teamwork structures

Teamwork may be seen as a response to the perceived complexities of the contemporary working environment; the increased digitalization of the workplace may well have contributed to this by generating a requirement for increased flexibilization, and this may well have given rise to the emergence of teams beyond the co-located structure. These newer types of teams are referred to as dispersed or virtual teams, which are not fixed in time or space, or as networked teams that may comprise different teams organized in multisystem formats. It seems highly likely that an increasingly significant part of the collective working reality is the requirement to manage and lead these newer types of teams. This is problematic for practicing leaders as the theories associated with the leadership of these teams lag behind the incidence of practice. Nevertheless, consideration ought to be given to three developments in leadership theory: namely, a networked approach, systems leadership and distributed leadership, as these have something important to say about the new working realities for leaders.

## The networked approach to leadership

It would help here to establish an understanding of what is meant by networks and the essential principles for network functioning, despite the view that due to increased utilization of networked platforms there exists an awareness of how they operate. However, in organizational and social lives, much is taken for granted as patterns of behavior and norms are adhered to principally through habit. Consequently, little attempt is made to think about them in a critical way by asking questions about what is understood and, more importantly, how individuals have come to understand what they understand. However, possibly as a consequence of the frequency of network platforms, a networked way of thinking has become increasingly more apparent. Networks themselves are not new and are not limited to the digital platforms that are commonplace; they have always existed as a central feature of social relations, and there is a resonance between networking and the social relationship within leadership.

In the networked approach, according to Kilduff, Tsai and Hanke (2006), there are broadly four interrelated principles that set this approach apart from other competing perspectives. These are as follows: the importance of social relations between members of the network; the extent to which the individual is embedded within the network; the utility of network connections; the structures and patterns of social life. In themselves, some of these principles seem quite abstract and therefore warrant an explanation.

The first of these is the most straightforward. Within social networks, it is the relationships between individual actors, as opposed to the attributes of the individual actor, that are of significance. This is entirely in line with our definition of leadership and also forms an essential strand of particular leadership approaches, such as the leader-member exchange (LMX) theory (See Martin et al., 2010).

The second principle needs to be appreciated as the extent to which the actor is embedded in networks of human social relations. Underlying this is the consideration that actors prefer to interact with those who are within a community as opposed to those outside it. This in turn is based on the assumption that people have a tendency to enter into relationships with friends, family and others known to them as opposed to complete strangers. There is an emphasis here on people's perceptions of others in that these are reflected in the extended relationships they hold. As an example, a person's perception of me may reflect the relationship I hold with my coworkers or my direct line manager – the extent to which the perception of my relationships with others affects the relationship with another is embeddedness. From a leadership perspective the effectiveness of me as a leader therefore may well depend upon the perceptions of the relationships I have with others in the network.

The third principle is that the relationships held within the network provide a value (utility) to the participants and to the community. Dependent on the various arrangements of the relationships in the network, the amount of value may differ. (It important to note that this does not refer exclusively to economic value.) At the team level, the value extracted may result in the group formally recognizing itself as a team and its capacity to become an effective team. This shows that an outcome of the network might be that the group produces sufficient value to reconstitute itself as a team and begins to work accordingly. Additionally, the same principle is concerned with the migratory effects of leadership across hierarchies and functional boundaries.

The fourth and final principal is concerned with 'structural patterning.' This is a complex dynamic that focuses on the underlying structural factors that shape relationships between individuals beyond a simple description. This alone has a correspondence with leadership, as the structuring of the task and teams is an essential part of situational or contingency leadership. Whilst the description may prove an effective jumping off point, what is of interest here is the way in which two people may be able to reach each other through the shortest number of connections or ties between individuals who are within the network. This may prove to be helpful in establishing who exactly is leading in a given moment by looking at the relative social structures within which individuals are located.

In network terms therefore leadership is framed around these four principles and, according to Pastor, Meindl and Mayo (2002), leadership should be seen less as a collection of attributes held by the individual and more as a product of the social capital held by the network, and it is this that comprises the important distinction found within this perspective. Leadership is determined as a collective function of the social capital within the group. Individuals may invest time in developing the quality of their social relationships and in adding to (and eliminating) the number of network members in order to enhance their own social capital. In addition, there is a strong element of cooperation required because seeing group working as a zero-sum game does not enhance the network. The network is developed as a consequence of social ties, so one needs to give as much to contributing to relationships as will benefit all of the parties. There is a strong element of paradox as, whilst the social structure of the network (organization) provides opportunities for leaders, the same social structure is not under the control of any one particular individual.

As an illustration of this, the 'ripple effect' with respect to the leadership of teams should be examined, particularly for those who are not co-located. Imagine someone within a network seeking to develop and extend his or her relations and equate this with dropping a pebble into a still pond. The concentric ripples radiate outward and can in turn be shaped by other ripples that spread from others doing exactly the same thing. The patterns, both on the surface and below the waterline, are complex and dependent upon who does what, and are in essence beyond the control of the individual. Nevertheless, the intricacy and complexity of the patterns of ripples can throw out some very interesting and opportune shapes that may comprise opportunities to lead and, more importantly, opportunities to develop leadership practice. The emergence of leadership within complex patterns of relationships therefore may seem to be overtly reliant upon luck, and here I am reminded of the quote attributed to the golfer, Gary Player.

## "The more I practice, the luckier I get."

What is being suggested here is that working in order to maximize our own practice provides opportunities that to others may be perceived as luck. Consequently, whilst individuals cannot control their own social networks, they can definitely enhance them and can most certainly detrimentally impact the network. At the center of the network exists social capital as a function of human relations, and this can be promoted through utilizing and developing the social skills that we possess. Heifitiz and Laurie (2001) use the metaphor of the dance hall to make tangible the abstract under consideration here. Not only are individuals required to be on the dance floor but also they need to be mindful to visit the balcony from time to time to witness the patterns of the dances occurring below; note that this activity is both strategic and deliberate.

## The systems approach to leadership

Potentially this area of theorizing could prove to be very fruitful, but for this to occur a distancing from functional perspectives of leadership would need to occur. Where one remains wedded to assumptions of leadership as a functional response to organizational problems and the delivery of solutions without consideration of the wider dynamics of character, personality, psyche and the critical social dimensions of human interaction, one remains tied to the importance of the individual leader as paramount. At its very worst, systems leadership is presented as providing the resolution of complex organizational problems without considering what those processes of leadership might entail. This is at best lazy scholarship and at worst lacks any utility as it ignores the vital and unique element of complexity by conflating it with the merely complicated and ignores the phenomenon of emergence in any material way.

This concept of emergence has been popularized by the maxim coined by Lorenz that suggests the flapping of a butterfly's wings in the Amazon basin could cause a hurricane in the USA; the consequence of seemingly small events can generate unprecedented and unforeseen consequences elsewhere. The application of complexity thinking to the subjective social world may be less straightforward as it may not be possible to rely on the methods of natural science, but nevertheless, the principles of emergence remain consistent. The task of the leader is more to facilitate processes of emergence to occur as opposed to take the central position and lead the team (or organization) toward its objective. Any action by the nominal leader has the potential to equally be detrimental, and it is worth considering this in terms of the perceived efficacy attributed to the individual leader.

This new emphasis on a virtual or networked realm that is not constrained by time and geography gives credence to a development of leadership that has become known as shared or distributed leadership, a perceived superior framing of leadership as here everyone can and should be a leader. In this current context, the group shares the leadership role, a possibility that was noted by Gibb (1954), who saw leadership as a shared quality. However, the concept of distributed or shared leadership, whilst a relatively new development, is still dominated by the functional approaches that preceded it. Effectively, leadership is stored in one person who 'shares' it with others; this is clearly not a true distribution of leadership. Similarly, leaders require other individuals to be led; if everyone is a leader, who exactly is being led? Furthermore, the task may prove Intractable and, according to Grint (2005), in such circumstances it is likely that someone will opt to command and appoint other commanders to the subtext of the problem. Again, this is not distributed leadership as conceptualized. Whilst this framing of leadership is gaining increased popularity amongst various types of organizations, the view of leadership as a distributed phenomenon is more theoretical than observed.

Perhaps the biggest problem within this topic of team leadership under a functional spotlight is that the definition of what constitutes a team is so restrictive that the kind of leadership required to make the team more effective is, by nature of the definition, quite rare. It is claimed that there are many more pseudo teams in an organization than there are real teams, but could this be because, in attempting to resolve the leadership of teams' conundrum, it is concluded that real teams are a result of good leadership and that pseudo teams (the majority), by definition bad (or less effective) teams, must lack good leadership. In essence, because the pseudo teams do not fit the model, they can effectively be discounted, despite their being the norm and focus therefore on the minority that demonstrates the value of teams and the associated leadership. This could be seen as an example of what Gemmill and Oakley (1992) have described as an alienating social myth. The power of teams and leadership maintains its authority simply because it is an undiscussable part of our cultural beliefs and makeup. The authors suggest that a consequence of this is a process referred to as 'reification' within which mental abstractions are converted into objective reality, and it is to this particular appreciation of the way the social world and leadership are constructed that is turned to next.

## Reflexive questions

What is your experience with leading teams? What might constitute the principle issues of team leadership?

Does the structure of the team shape how you might lead it?

## References

Alvesson, M., Blom, M. and Sveningsson, S. (2017). *Reflexive leadership: Organising in an imperfect world*. London: Sage.

Burke, C.S., Diaz Granados, C.S. and Salas, E. (2011). Team leadership: A review and look ahead. In: A. Bryman, D. Collinson, B. Jackson, K. Grint, and M. Uhl-Bien, eds., *The Sage handbook of leadership*. London: Sage.

Fiedler, F.E. (1967). *A theory of leadership effectiveness*. New York: McGraw-Hill.

Freud, S. (1921). *Group psychology and the analysis of the ego. The standard edition of the complete psychological works of Sigmund Freud, volume XVIII (1920–1922): Beyond the pleasure principle, group psychology and other works*. London: Hogarth Press, pp. 65–144.

Gemmill, G. and Oakley, J. (1997). Leadership: An alienating social myth. In: Grint K., ed., *Leadership: Classical, contemporary and critical approaches*. Oxford: Oxford University Press.

Gibb, C.A. (1954). Leadership. In: G. Lindzey, ed., *Handbook of social psychology*. Vol. 2. Reading: Addison-Wesley, pp. 877–917.

Grint, K. (2005). Problems, problems, problems: The social construction of 'leadership.' *Human Relations*, 58(11), pp. 1467–1494.

Heifetz, R. and Laurie, D.L. (2001). The work of leadership. *Harvard Business Review*, Dec. 2001.

Kilduff, M., Tsai, W. and Hanke, R. (2006). A paradigm too far? A dynamic stability reconsideration of the social network research program. *Academy of Management Review*, 31(4), pp. 1031–1048.

Marion, R. (1999). *The edge of organization: Chaos and complexity theories of formal social organizations*. Newbury Park, CA: Sage.

Pastor, J-C., Meindl, J.R. and Mayo, M.C. (2002). A network effects model of charisma attributions. *Academy of Management Journal*, 45(2), pp. 410–420.

Stacey, R.D., Griffin, D. and Shaw, P. (1999). *Complexity and management fad or radical challenge to systems thinking?* London: Routledge.

# 4 Social constructionism, stories and culture

To this point I have mainly considered approaches that may be defined as leader-centric where the leader is presented as the most important constituent of the leadership relationship. Clearly the leader is important, but it might be suggested that the efficacy and potency of the individual is overstated when considered alongside the potential impact of other dynamics inherent in the leadership phenomenon. This chapter presents a significant alternative that challenges the leader-centric approach to provide much-needed balance by locating the leader in a wider, more social context. This chapter is broken down into three sections. In the first short section, social constructionism is outlined as a method of social inquiry. Secondly, the relevance of a social constructivist approach is aligned with leadership thinking by considering leadership stories and language. Finally, the first two parts of the chapter are applied to organizational culture with the associated implications for leadership practice.

## Social constructionism

The social constructivist approach is a method for thinking about and analyzing wider society, the conceptual antecedents of which can be found in more interpretivist social accounts and stand against the methods of inquiry outlined in the earlier chapters. Importantly, social constructionism doesn't determine a specific approach but comprises an array of techniques that can broadly be classified with a concern for highlighting the processes by which people construct and co-construct the world in which they and others reside. Consequently, they are informed by the foundations provided by many contributors from a variety of fields.[1,2] It is with the seminal publication by Berger and Luckman (1966) that a wider acknowledgment and application to an array of topics that cover management and organization, including leadership, is made. Many of the texts associated with social constructionism are difficult to follow as they are mired in the philosophical terminology required to explain shared lived realities. Reality, as a consequence, is not an objective 'something' to be uncovered through scientific inquiry but should be more appreciated as multiple competing realities about what constitutes the true and legitimate. Material or otherwise, these realities are constructed through social processes in which meanings are negotiated, constructed, challenged and established iteratively over time. Given the emphasis on social interaction, it's of little surprise therefore that the approach centers on the use and role of language and communication. Most social constructionist scholars hold the view that language does not just mirror reality but actually constitutes it.

The consequences of this are therefore stark; language is not just an issue of transmission and reception, but it is also a medium through which the meaning is fashioned and given substance. Consider the following populist truism as applied to leadership: "actions speak louder than words." However, a social constructionist account may well assert the contrary, that "words speak louder than actions."

## Social constructionism in leadership: language and stories

There has grown in recent times a significant, if somewhat slightly confusing, literature concerning the social construction of leadership. Nevertheless, the intent, despite the various approaches, is the same: to understand the social phenomena under inquiry. What appears to be a difficult process might be better suited to those engaged in the scientific study of social systems with less benefit to aspiring leaders seeking to develop their own practice. Consequently, this may prove to be a challenge for practicing managers who are focused primarily on doing material things well. I strongly assert that negotiating the abstract is an essential process of reflecting on leadership in order to challenge, and ultimately improve, individual practice.

Social constructionist approaches to leadership generally exhibit two common considerations. The first is that they tend not to associate themselves with leader-centric perspectives within which the leader's personality and/or behavior is the primary determining influence on self, others and outcomes. Social constructionist approaches, however, would suggest that all members of the organization, regardless of how they came to be part of a leadership relationship, have the ability to make their own meanings and therefore are not reliant upon the notional leader figure to do it for them. The second commonality concerns leadership as a co-constructed reality that may be summarized as an "eye of the beholder" view; leadership is a phenomenon determined through the processes and outcomes of the necessary social interactions between people. In essence, discussion, discourse, stories and other symbolic media essential to context are the dynamics that bring about a particular form of leadership. Consequently, what is seen to be important and appropriate to leading is not a matter that can be predetermined by any objective criteria, as the situation itself is dependent upon the interpretation of those involved. This leads to the possibility that, in any given situation, accounts of the situation may well differ and also that the leader's own account is equally open to interpretation and may not be a reflection on what comprises 'true' leadership.

To illustrate this it is helpful to refer to Grint (2005), where a social constructionist account of leadership and context stands in contrast to the contingency approaches outlined elsewhere. There are a number of significant weaknesses concerning the inclusion of context into the leadership challenge, many of which stem from the rigid forms of taxonomy that seek to define context, in that they are inadequate in accurately defining the complexity of lived experiences. Grint redefines context by employing the tame-wicked classification of problems originally set out by Rittel and Webber (1973), by suggesting that there are generalist typologies of problems that establish the necessity for leadership in particular circumstances.

A 'tame' problem is one that has been seen before and consequently a previously applied and known solution is immediately available to the leader. A 'wicked' problem, on the other hand, comprises one that is novel and consequently intractable; the solution is not known and/or not readily available. In such a situation, Grint suggests it is highly probable that a leader, in the midst of an intractable problem, will treat it like, but not identical to, a previously known problem and will behave in a way that is perceived by themselves as appropriate. This gives rise to a third kind of problem as the wicked problem, as a consequence of the initial response, now descends into a crisis that demands that someone take control of the situation and begin to command. The point here is that the leader who takes command of a situation that may be determined to be wicked is not only likely to fail to resolve the problem but equally generates a crisis that is solvable by the command that was instrumental in creating the crisis in the first place. Grint's application of a social constructionist perspective to the understanding of the problem necessitates considering many accounts of the same situation and through synthesis arrives at an appropriate response. The appropriate response to an intractable problem is determined by accounts of the problem, which in turn gives rise to a collaborative agreed response – this he defines as 'leadership.'

Briefly, some consideration ought to be given to the irony implied by this analysis when related to other more normative approaches to leadership. Is someone taking control and command of the situation the very definition of what may commonly be referred to as 'strong' leadership? If this is the case, then it's interesting to suggest that the very notion of strong leadership is invariably exactly what is not required. Additionally, let's consider for a minute here the frequency of the various types of leader response. As Grint suggests, it is easier for an individual to take control and command the situation as opposed to genuinely lead; then the most common form of empirical leadership behavior is exactly the one that corresponds to the explicit use of coercive power. This has further implications in that organizations, by favoring strong leadership, may well be providing exactly the right structures for individuals who have a propensity to command, which may well be the wrong kind of leadership but also the wrong kind of individual to put into a leadership role. Furthermore, with reference to Freud's thinking on groups, the emergence of a leader at a time of crisis is someone who is a 'father figure,' strong enough to curtail anxiety and keep people safe. Consequently, the combination of the organization and the people within it foster and promote the need for a strong leader when affronted by external challenge to the organization. This provides some insight into the popularity and prevalence of the hero and heroic frames of leadership.

A second social constructionist account is outlined in Rosenzweig (2007), who provides a very interesting insight into how such accounts of leadership might function through the concept of halos that illustrates the power of leadership stories. Rosenzweig defines the halo effect as follows:

> The Halo Effect is a way for the mind to create and maintain a coherent and consistent picture, to reduce cognitive dissonance. The Halo Effect is just too strong, the desire to tell a coherent story too great, the tendency to jump on bandwagons too appealing.
>
> Rosenzweig (2014, p. 50)

> So many of the things we – managers, journalists, professors, and consultants commonly think contribute to company performance are often attributions based on performance.
>
> Rosenzweig (2014, p. 64)

The assertions here are that people have the capacity to not only create stories that generate halos but also stories that constitute them, which leads to a process whereby individuals are less capable of seeing reality as a consequence of halos and distorting 'delusions.' This last bit is probably the weakness in the overall thesis, as the delusions to which the author refers are constituent parts of our own realities. In other words, whoever has the most convincing narrative constitutes a collective reality.

The case of Jack Welsh and General Electric has been well documented by Froud et al. (2006) as one of a number of detailed case studies that outlines the response by corporate leaders to the requirements of financial markets to conclude that management agency is in effect limited and to a greater extent determined by the rise and fall of the same markets. Here the manager is required to craft a narrative that explains the discrepancies between performance and expectation; failure to do so can result in catastrophic collapses in stock market valuation. In the case of Jack Welsh, he took over as CEO of General Electric (GE) in 1981 and stayed until 2001, during which time the value of GE's stock had risen 4000%, or had gone from being a $12 billion company to being a $410 billion company, when he retired. It has been suggested by commentators on the success of GE that much of the firm's success is a consequence of the superior leadership exhibited by Welsh and his senior team, a style of leadership that was responsible for the design and implementation of a wholly dynamic organizational culture complemented by 'work around' problem-solving sessions, the productive application of six sigma and GE training and development programs, all of which contributed to *Fortune* magazine recognizing Welsh as the manager of the century. Froud et al. (2006) suggest that from a cultural economy perspective the narratives of Welsh and colleagues and the contributing commentary on the successes of the company have in effect 'performed' reality, that the accepted reasons for the success of GE are as a consequence of the narratives and stories about the reasons for its success; they have been constituted by the exact same narratives and stories.

It can be taken from this that the importance of the leader's ability to craft a narrative/story has the ability to reframe the understanding of others. Leaders, and in particular senior leaders, have an elevated authority and substance that makes their stories more appealing, more compelling and therefore something that constitutes our lived realities. In effect, leadership stories might be considered as attributions after the fact, and as a consequence, they have the ability to obscure reality and in its place craft a new accepted frame for our experiences. Consider the justification for new visions as examinations of past performances, the rationale of why something worked and/or failed, all of these are well intentioned and wholeheartedly believed, but as a consequence of our own delusions and biases, they are probably best perceived as sincere lies, not intentional mistruths but realistic narratives in support of individual leadership capability.

An assumption made here is that language has the capacity to shape meaning and therefore the realities of individual lived experiences. A social constructionist account of leadership emphasizes the words leaders use, as these shape the realities of those that comprise the led. More commonly, within approaches that have a social constructionist core language, they may be referred to specifically as narratives or discourses, but in practice they mean the same thing. Language has a particular potency and resonance, as it is through this medium that humans recount their own experiences and understanding, which in turn influences the way that others think about their own circumstances. Reality is constructed by language, as in effect reality can only be that which is described by language. Within this frame therefore the language of leaders, who have obtained positions of authority and influence, possesses a particularly potent form of influence, and as a consequence, can and will shape the meaning and the realities of those they are charged to lead. It should be apparent that leadership stories might be seen as an important contributor not only to leadership performance but also, just as critically, to the perception of leadership performance.

Smircich and Morgan (1982) published one of the most important pieces of work on leadership, but it has received less consideration than perhaps it ought. There are a number of interesting things about the paper itself, the first of which is the title, "Leadership: The management of meaning," which clearly refers to leadership *and* management and suggests a close relationship between the two; one ought to be managing one's leadership. This goes against much of our assumed knowledge concerning leadership and management in that they are more traditionally thought of as separate and very different processes. The authors start from normative perceptions of both leadership and management to suggest that leadership has the capacity to inspire novel approaches to problems and generate outcomes above and beyond the mundane practices of management. Leadership somehow is more desirable, although abstract, is egalitarian and is within our own agency. Management relies upon formal hierarchical structures and is therefore authoritarian and routed in the relations of power between the managed and the manager. However, Smirch and Morgan suggest that leadership can be and ought to be managed and that leadership itself is routed in the same authoritarian processes. Leaders have power; the led do not. Ultimately, therefore, the expression of a particular perspective in giving sense to what is/has or will occur is a managed demonstration of the leader's power; in other words, the story being disseminated has a foundation in both formal and informal bases of power and becomes established as the 'true' account of the experience.

I think this has important implications when consideration is given to the leadership stories of those regarded as authentic leaders, or indeed for us in our attempts to be genuinely authentic. In other chapters, I have suggested the idea that authenticity is problematic, as each of us holds a multiplicity of selves and identities, all of which demand a different kind of focus and agency. Can leadership stories therefore genuinely be authentic, or are they motivated by any number of different factors, from the situation and context of those being led to individual psyche and character? Would a genuinely authentic leader admit to the confusion inherent within their own stories and consequent halos, and would this by consequence diminish their leadership in the eyes of those being led?

When considering language and its use in leadership, it is important to consider the actual language that is employed to describe leaders and leadership, particularly when one considers the utilization of a heavily gendered frame of language that tends to be deployed when describing leaders and the leadership being demonstrated. Does the language used to describe either the skills or competencies of a particular leadership framework heavily slant toward a masculine bias, words such as 'decisive,' 'powerful,' 'competitive,' 'driven,' and as a consequence, therefore, does the common usage of such language impose upon others a particular form of behavior, where alternative forms of behavior and language are either less valued or treated pejoratively. Of course, it may well be that the use of certain language has become more gender neutral over time. As an example, both genders may be considered to be 'strong,' but does a 'strong woman' and a 'strong man' mean the same thing? I would argue that it doesn't if one allows oneself to focus on the imagery that is generated by both terms. Furthermore, which determination holds the higher currency or is most valued within the organization? A more critical examination of the language used needs to be given; for example, the word 'achieve' generally may be perceived as a masculine term, but it doesn't necessarily follow that women do not or cannot achieve. However, in any particular context, does the method of achieving align more with a particular gender and their methods of achieving?

## Leadership and culture

To some extent the work of Edgar Schein on organizational culture and leadership illustrates the trajectory of conceptual development illustrated in this chapter so far. In early formative thinking, like much of leadership thinking of the time, the role between leadership and culture is seen as being functionally oriented. As an example, Bennis (1979) expresses the view that the primary role of the leader in crafting the culture of work is the critical difference between leadership and management. In the first edition of the book, Schein (1985) maintains a close affinity with the work of contemporary writers by establishing the leader as the architect of organizational culture and develops his thoughts further than most by tying organizational culture and leadership closely together. Firstly, he maintains that leadership is the essential process through which culture is originated, and secondly, he sees manipulation of culture as the unique function of leaders and their leadership.

The real differentiator between Schein's approach relative to others is that whilst apparently suggesting that the structuring of organizational culture is relatively straightforward, Schein acknowledges the potential complexity by suggesting that the definitions and construction of both leadership and culture are difficult; the combination of both in terms of what they comprise and how they may impact each other increases the complexity and therefore levels of uncertainty.

By the fifth edition, Schein (2017) reaffirms his view with respect to culture formation by arguing that it is the founders of the business who establish the culture. Whilst this may be true, it isn't very helpful when one may be the latest in a very long line of leaders who have previously held the position. Schein acknowledges this, and in doing so, he seemingly confirms that the individual has less of an impact than the earlier set of leaders; he similarly maintains that leaders are organizational entrepreneurs, the architects of culture, and can influence what kind of culture is exhibited in the organization. Additionally, leaders have a particular responsibility to speed up cultural change when and if the culture itself becomes problematic. In doing this, leaders focus on the foundations of culture which are established between the interplay of three sets of variables.

The first set of variables is classed as 'artifacts,' defined as visible representations of the culture that may be noticed by an outsider. The second are referred to as 'values,' and it these that reflect the higher levels of organizational consciousness. In essence, they reflect how things should be. The final class of variables is 'assumptions'; these are beliefs about the organization that are taken to be true. When these are understood, any confusion concerning the contradictions between values and artifacts becomes more effectively resolved. In essence, the difference between Schein and many others' perspectives of culture is that Schein allocates the casual relationship to the assumptions that underpins all other variables, as it is the 'hidden' assumptions that are made material in the artifacts and values of the organization.

What is important here is the relative importance that Schein gives in later editions of his work to the artifacts of dialogue, speech and stories, and it is this that directly links this approach to a social constructionist perspective. Culture therefore should not be seen as some common monolith across the organization; culture is by its very nature flexible and fragmentary. Not only can leaders shape cultural assumptions through their actions and their narratives but also the leader may in turn be shaped by the culture in which they work; the relationship of culture and leadership should not be seen as unidirectional. Whilst a ready acceptance of the view that leaders shape organizational culture may be given, equally if an acceptance that causality runs in both directions is made, then it must be that culture shapes leaders and their leadership.

A consideration of the co-construction of culture in its practical terms provides us with an understanding of why leadership capability is not always transferable between different organizations and contexts. It is not a given therefore that the success of a leader in any particular organization may be replicated in any other, as the context, the interpretations of context and the language used are full of explicit and implicit meanings and will also be different. This, logically, according to Fairhurst and Grant (2010), suggests that a social constructionist position on leadership ought to take into account that leadership need not have existed or need not be all that it is deemed to be; leadership is not determined by the nature of things and is therefore not inevitable. More provocatively, this can be taken further in that leadership, as suggested by Grint (2005), can be detrimental and inhibiting, and it might be better if leadership as traditionally considered were done away with or at least transformed into something else.

## Reflexive questions

Reflect upon your workplace: what halos do you see? How are they constituted, and what is their effect?

Spend some time reflecting upon your own use of language in a particular instance when you think your choice of language was appropriate and effective. What exactly contributed to its effectiveness?

## Notes

1  George Herbert Mead (1863–1931) is generally considered to be the founder of symbolic interactionism. Mead was very strongly influenced by American pragmatism and consequently saw people as social products but that they are primarily purposive and creative; consequently, the truth of the theory resides in the way it is useful in solving complex human problems. Despite the esteem with which other scholars regard Mead, he never actually set out the core of his ideas or the processes within which they may be made real. Students of Mead pulled together the lectures and teaching notes that had been so formative, influencing a generation of the best minds in thinking about sociology, and published *Mind, Self and Society* in his name posthumously (which is rather ironic). According to Mead, the 'mind' of the title is concerned with the individual's capacity to use symbols to create meaning about the world within which the individual lives. Individuals use language and thought (and thoughts on language) in order to accomplish this. 'Self' refers to the ability of the individual to reflect upon the way others perceive them, and 'society' is the space where these interactions take place. Symbolic interactionism asserts that physical reality exists, but it is determined

by individual social definitions and that these develop as a consequence of individual ability to filter individual and conflicting perceptions of what constitutes
the real.

2 Alfred Schutz (1899–1959) was a student of Edmund Husserl, the founder of
phenomenological thought, which may be defined as the study of things as they
appear (as phenomena). This may be seen as a more descriptive than explanatory
form of thought. The project of phenomenologists is to provide a clear and undis-
torted account of the way things are. Much of Schutz's work comprises a study
on the way(s) in which individuals use everyday ordinary interactions to produce
a feeling of reality and intersubjectivity. The two authors of the formative text on
social constructionism referred to here are probably the most noted scholars influenced by Schultz's work, despite the apparent significant differences on beliefs
and natural attitude.

# References

Bennis, W. (1976). Leadership: A beleaguered species? *Organizational dynamics.*
Vol. 5, pp. 3–16.

Berger, P.L. and Luckmann, T. (1966). *The social construction of reality: A treatise
in the sociology of knowledge.* New York: Anchor.

Fairhurst, G.T. and Grant, D. (2010). The social construction of leadership: A sailing
guide. *Management Communication Quarterly*, 24(2), pp. 171–210.

Froud, J., Johal, S., Leaver, A. and Williams, K. (2006). *Financialization and strat-
egy: Narrative and numbers.* London: Routledge.

Grint, K. (2005). Problems, problems, problems: The social construction of 'leadership.' *Human Relations*, 58(11), pp. 1467–1494.

Mead, G.H. (1934). *Mind self and society.* Chicago, IL: University of Chicago Press.

Rittel, H.W.J. and Weber, M.M. (1973). Dilemmas in a general theory of planning.
*Policy Sciences*, 4(2), pp. 155–169.

Rosenzweig's, P. (2014). *The halo effect.* 2nd ed. London: Simon & Schuster.

Schien, E. (1985). *Organizational culture and leadership.* 1st ed. San Francisco:
Jossey Bass.

Schien, E. (2017). *Organizational culture and leadership.* 5th ed. San Francisco:
Jossey Bass.

Shutz, A. (1970). *On phenomenology and social relations: Selected writings.* Edited
by Helmut R. Wagner. Chicago, IL: University of Chicago Press.

Smirchich, L. and Morgan, G. (1982). Leadership: The management of meaning.
*The Journal of Applied Behavioral Science*, 18(3), pp. 257–273.

Yukl, G. (2011). Contingency theories of effective leadership. In: A. Bryman, D.
Collinson, G. Grint, and M. Uhl-Bien, eds., *The Sage handbook of leadership.*
London: Sage.

# 5  Followers and leadership

A definition of leadership is as follows: 'Follow me,' which is inter-esting for a number of reasons but particularly because the follower comes first. The following is qualified by the object to be followed – "Me", referring to the leader, and again, a simple statement such as this sets out the central importance of the leader but at least acknowl-edges, I think, the involvement of followers. There are a few points on which leadership scholars agree, but one of them may be that, in order to exist as a leader, followers are required. The essence of leadership therefore is following. There can be no leader without followers, but whilst leaders may have subordinates, this doesn't necessarily make them followers. In the first part of this chapter, followers in the leader-ship phenomenon are considered. Next, specific follower-centric per-spectives are considered before the implications for practicing leaders are explored.

## Following in the leadership literature

The literature on following can be considered to be a wide-ranging spec-trum. At one end, the role of followers has been underplayed, if not ignored, most likely due to the dominance of neo-charismatic studies since the early 1980s. These have typically focused on top leadership teams to develop highly focused leader-centric models, which consequently view leadership as a top-down process between the leader and subordinate. Here leaders are set apart by their ability to mobilize and bring about elevated performances of followers. Later developments, such as the full range leadership theory, continue to assert this, stating that the transformational leader focuses on the material needs of the follower and is able to build on the follower's self-concept and worth, to mold an identity that reflects the leader's own self-concept and mission. Followers are being presented both individually and collectively as passive subjects to be shaped, influenced and coerced by the leader. The relationship between leaders and followers is therefore essentially a linear, one-way relationship from the leader to follower, but as was shown in the previous chapter, in a socially constructed world, this might not be the case.

Alternatively, at the opposite end of the spectrum sits a variety of contributions that maintain that followers have a vital but varied role to play in the leadership process; some oppose the notion of followers as docile and have sought to state their individual and collective value. As a consequence, the currency of followers has become vitalized as the traditional is challenged. Indeed, it would be remiss not to acknowledge that a more integral role for followers is to be found in some reworking of earlier material, an example of which would be Avolio (2011), who emphasizes leadership as a systemic process within which the quality of relationships between leaders and followers is seen as critical.

Not surprisingly for a contested concept, the value of followers and the role they play in the leadership relationship has been outlined in a number of ways, depending on the relative importance that followers are given in the leader-follower dynamic. Important work by Jeffrey Meindl (1990) paved the way by identifying the romantic foundations of leadership, whilst Jackson and Parry (2008) further outline three distinct follower-centric perspectives,[1] where followers may be seen as moderators, substitutes and constructors of leadership.

## Romance

A concern that leadership had become overly preoccupied with leader-centric views of leadership, led to the perception that it was in turn perpetuating the hype and unrealistic expectation that is routinely placed upon leaders and became a focus for Meindl and associates and to an extent marked the beginning of a genuinely follower-centric model of leadership. Whilst not seeking to minimize or undermine the role of leaders, Meindl (1990) notably remarked that "it is easier to believe in leadership than prove it" (Meindl, 1990, p. 161). This quote follows an extensive archival project that looked at specific cases of leadership in practice to show that leadership had frequently been used when explaining both good and bad outcomes of organizational functioning. People were more favorable toward successful outcomes when they were associated with leadership where any personal shortcoming is likely to be overlooked in deference to the positive outlook. The convincing evidence provided by Meindl, particularly when aligned with the halo effect discussed in Chapter 4, demonstrates that there is a strong belief, bordering on faith, in the importance of leadership to the functioning of organized systems. Furthermore, this supports the attribution of qualities in which leadership is appreciated in terms of an overtly romanticized function of individuals and competencies, mostly working at senior parts of the organization's hierarchy. Followers readily ascribe a causal responsibility to leaders with the events that might plausibly be linked to them. In effect, leadership acts as a simplified, biased but attractive way to explain organizational performance, particularly in cases seen at the extreme ends of performance and outcomes.

Meindl describes the romance of leadership as a social construction; followers construct an opinion concerning a leader through interacting with other followers, facilitating a process of 'social contagion,' which might be thought of as being similar to the spread of a socially derived and constrained virus spread from follower to follower until a significant persuasive group becomes infected. Social contagion really highlights the interpersonal processes and group dynamics that underpin the widespread dissemination of not only the 'charisma' of leaders but also the very core of the interpersonal influence relationship that may be seen to typify leadership.

## Social identity theory

Within social identity theory, leadership is confirmed as primarily a social process in which leaders are able to persuade others to embrace new values, attitudes and goals, and to exert additional effort in the achievement of those goals. The theory proposes that the extent to which an individual is accepted as a leader depends upon how "prototypical" (or representative) the individual is of the group. Whilst it may well be that prototypicality should not be considered as the sole reason for establishing leadership, where a leader attracts followers who share a similar background and beliefs, but also the reverse process is possible, whereby the leader is selected and supported by followers because the leader is like the group in terms of characteristics, beliefs, aspirations and values. In the absence of a leader who is prototypical of the group, group members will use generalized information to create an impression (stereotype) of the person involved.

Referring back to team leadership, it may be that leadership and identity are mutually interdependent features of social group life. Leadership is dependent on group members sharing a social identity where leaders play a fundamental part in the construction of that identity. Whilst the main focus of this work is on the leader's identity, there is some complementary interest in the way that leaders influence followers' identity as an indirect means of increasing commitment. Whilst traditional leadership models are often seen as a form of zero-sum game, that leader agency can be achieved only at the expense of follower agency; it may be argued that the agencies of leaders and followers are interdependent to the extent that they rely upon each other to create the conditions where mutual influence is possible, or in other words, socially constructed.

Collinson (2005) has gone some of the way to reducing many of the gaps identified in a fuller appreciation of social identity theory and leadership. He maintains that studies of leadership need to develop a broader and deeper understanding of followers' identities and rejects the idea that the identities of followers are homogenous. Collinson's approach suggests that followers' identities are likely to be much more complex and differentiated than previously thought. Individuals are best understood as 'social selves' whose actions have to be understood within their own social environment. Whilst some identities are mutually reinforcing, others may be in tension, mutually contradictory and even incompatible. Organizations not only produce products and services, but, in important symbolic and material ways, they also produce people capable of differing responses to leadership. At any one time, someone with a degree of accountability within an organization will be a leader, follower and manager, and within this framework, the possibility of conflict and dilemmas as to how one might best respond is less than straightforward.

## Follower-centric perspectives: followers as moderators of leadership

In this first follower-centric perspective, followers are positioned in their mainly passive role as receivers of leadership influence, but it does acknowledge, at least, that the leader's influence may have to vary depending on the constituency of the follower(s) being addressed. Here the view sits comfortably with contingency theorists of leadership but is also relevant when considering aspects of neo-charismatic models. It is recognized that the approach of the leader may have to be moderated in order to appeal to the follower. Those leaders designated as transformational,

> diagnose the needs of their followers and then elevate those needs to initiate and promote development.
>
> Bass and Avolio (1994, p. 552)

This, along with the transformational criteria of "individualized consideration," requires that there is some modification of the approach to the individual follower. Furthermore, deliberation must also be given to the criteria of "idealized influence," or charisma. This is specifically so if charisma is seen as being a construct that is not contained as a trait within the individual leader, as asserted by Bryman (1993). Here the generation of appeal between leaders and followers is derived as a result of the different approaches used, consciously or otherwise, in order to develop the desired response. The assertion that a manager's career successes and failures may be attributed to levels of interpersonal skills is given a high degree of credibility by Martin (2012).

In the earlier theorizing, transforming behavior was seen as superior to its transactional counterpart. Within the full range leadership model, however, the value of transactional behaviors became more appreciated and central to the overall leadership approach. The best leaders employ both transformational and transactional behaviors dependent upon the follower. Within this, the negotiation of transactional benefits between the leader and follower demands a modified approach to the individual and therefore to the overall practice of leadership.

The division between transformational and transactional behaviors may be less clear-cut than neo-charismatic scholars would assert, and certainly the contribution of transactional behaviors may have been overlooked in effectively practicing leadership. To some extent this may be because transactional behaviors have become synonymous with management; however, making a clear definitional difference between leadership and management is also problematic. According to Rost, much of leadership theorizing is indistinct and weak in definition, and consequently the two terms are conflated. He suggests therefore that much of what has been thought to be leadership is, in fact, effective general management. After all, any sentence within which the words management and leadership are interchangeable without fundamentally changing the meaning of the original sentence may lead us to suggest that we are referring to the same thing. Might a moderated approach therefore be seen as the management of leadership?

## Follower-centric perspectives: followers as substitutes for leadership

In the substitutes for leadership perspective, Kerr and Jermier (1978) maintain that a variety of organizational, group, task and individual factors are important in providing guidance to and good feelings for employees. Leadership behavior, as classically understood, can be important but should be examined in the context of other factors, some of which can be substituted for or neutralize the leader's influence. Included amongst these variables identified as potential substitutes for leadership are four groupings of subordinate characteristics (ability, experience, training and knowledge; need for independence; professional orientation; and indifference to organizational rewards); three task characteristics (task feedback; routine, methodologically invariant tasks; intrinsically satisfying tasks); and six organizational characteristics (organizational formalization; organizational inflexibility; group cohesiveness; amount of advisory/staff support; rewards outside the leader's control; and the degree of spatial distance between supervisors and subordinates).

Unlike the transformational approach to leadership, which assumes that the leader's transformational behavior is the key to improving leadership effectiveness, the substitutes for leadership approach assumes that the real key to leadership effectiveness is to identify those important situational or contextual variables that may "substitute" for the leader's behavior so that the leader can adapt his or her behavior accordingly. If the leader's influence is substituted, the possibility of leadership actually being evident must be considered, as the leader's activities are deemed largely irrelevant.

The theory has seemingly been developed with the aim of deemphasizing the role of the nominated leader and enhancing the role followers play within the relationship; nevertheless, empirical studies have failed to substantiate the substitutes theory to any satisfactory degree. This may be due to the consequence of seeing leadership as a function and/or a functional role. However, when seen as an influencing relationship where an individual exerts disproportionate coercive influence over others, this cannot therefore in essence be shared or substituted for. To my mind this is probably an overtly simplistic way of seeing leadership as being only one thing or another. Is there no possibility that leadership can be both a functional and interpersonal relationship? More recently, a couple of empirical studies, Evans, Hassard and Hyde (2013) and Empson (2017), have reported similar findings. Here both studies indicate that the dynamic of the relationship is complex and that factors within the dynamic give rise to the possibility of politics and professionalism being substitutes for leadership.

## Follower-centric perspectives: followers as constructors of leadership

In this perspective, leadership as a social relationship is central, and as a consequence, this suggests that both sides contribute to the formation of the relationship. Within a group of theories, referred to as leader-member exchange (LMX) theories (see Martin et al., 2010), researchers maintain that three elements need to be noted simultaneously: the leader, the follower and the relationship. More pertinently, leader behaviors and follower behaviors constitute the relationship. In other words, the relationship is co-constructed between both parties, and this has a significant degree of resonance to the social constructionist perspectives considered earlier. A question for consideration here is that in contributing to the construction of the leadership relationship, are followers engaging in what might be referred to as 'followership,' and might this be different from leadership, and if so, in what way? Rost argues that followers are an integral part of the relationship and are not engaging in followership, but if this is the case and they are engaging in leadership, who exactly are the followers?

## Followers and following in practice

It is asserted here that leadership theorizing does an injustice to the followers in the leadership relationship, as they are mostly overlooked and frequently regarded as unimportant. And yet, they are a central part of the relationship; after all, he who has no followers cannot be by any definition a leader at all. The leader, from their elevated position, is unlikely to be able to do the work of, say ten (subordinate), individuals, and below that ten there may reside another hundred and so on; it is the followers who will do the work, and hence they obtain their importance. This might, however, be part of the reasoning as to why the virtues of the leader and their leadership are extolled. As they are not in a position to be able to do the practical work of multiple people, leaders can lay claim to the importance of their visions and their motivational competences in order to get followers to do the work, a kind of 'added value' that complements the production of the 'real' value of goods and services that are bought or consumed, whether through appeal or necessity.

Moreover, the value of the many over the few is generally acknowledged in fields outside of work, such as politics, for example. Even within leadership itself, there is a view that is organized entirely around supporting the requirements of the many. Greenleaf (1970) introduced the notion of servant leadership, which in essence is the amalgamation in one body of two distinct facets: the leader who is trusted and shapes others' destinies, and the servant who, full of integrity, lifts people with the power of their own example. Despite the overtly spiritual overtones of this perspective, the focus here ought to be on the acknowledgment of the value of both constituent parts of the leadership relationship and the potentiality for both bodies should they work in tandem, in one individual or otherwise. Greenleaf's perspective was not new in the 1970s and can be traced back throughout the ages; consequently, this must raise a question as to why in contemporary framings of leadership, the follower has so roundly been ignored.

Leadership in and of itself, principally because of the currency with which it is held, is located at the exciting end of the organizational continuum; it's rather appealing to be considered a leader and be provided with an opportunity to become a better leader. It may well be that the narratives and stories, including the theories and concepts that dominate the framing of leadership, have 'performed' the perceptions of leaders and their leadership; they are important to the detriment of other facets of organization. Consider the aphorism of "If one leads, others must follow." This implies to an extent that there is an automatic compunction to follow the leader; it is difficult to resist. If there exists a romance about leadership, the same cannot be said of following. Here the follower is the *tabla rasa*, an empty vessel or blank slate upon which the leader writes their will. Clearly followers are not held in equivalent esteem. Followers – follow; the mere word itself implies that followers are of a lesser caliber than the leader. No one desires to become an accomplished follower, as the actual title itself is somehow demeaning, carries less weight and, whilst their importance is quietly acknowledged, there is no desire to be classed as one.

In any hierarchical organizational structure, there is only one formal leader (or a small group), and so by definition, the others must all be followers. This leads to an interesting conclusion in that all members of the organization must be both leader and follower, including the CEO, who must at least report to (follow) the board or report to a government agency or to whomever they owe money or the promise of return. Can you think of anyone who is only a 'leader' in that they have no following requirements; even in politics this rule holds true. The UK's prime minister follows to a greater or lesser extent parliament, the monarch, the executive branch and the electorate. This conundrum may well be coming clearer to US President Donald Trump, who probably held more autonomy in his corporate life than in his political life, as the US Constitution is designed to balance the various branches of government – so even the most powerful individual in the developed world is a follower. Safe in the knowledge therefore that the title of follower applies to everyone bar the most extreme dictators (corporate, political or otherwise) on the planet should make its acceptance easier.

Accepting therefore that each individual is a mix of follower and leader, consideration needs to be given to the requisite skills for both roles. Empirically, organizations and academics alike have focused on defining what constitutes skilled/effective performance at work, from leadership models to competency frameworks, and behavioral mapping to emotional competency frameworks. Irrespective of the view that many of these tend to be based on an ideal typology, and the small possibility that one individual holds all the relevant competences, should not diminish the view that they have been codified and hold great currency. But, as leaders are also followers, and I might argue that the majority of working time is spent following as opposed to leading, particularly in light of the definition provided in Chapter 1, what exactly is the difference in skills/competences between leaders and followers? Surely the same individual, in effect, is like the god Janus who has two heads; therefore, the skill requirements for the leader must be the same for a follower with some flux between the relative merits of various attributes. On this basis a follower development program might look exactly the same as a leader development program but with the added consequence of knowing that one is on the opposite side of the asymmetrical power relationship. This means that there exists the very tangible possibility that the follower must show more leadership ability than the nominal leader, as they do not have the same resources of power to draw upon. Could it be therefore that in order to become an adept leader, one must first become an equal and accomplished follower?

The concept of a skilled follower belies the logic of much of normative leadership theory, within which the follower is generally ignored or is seen as a passive party to the leadership relationship. However, the consideration of skills that constitute the follower would seem to imply that there is judgment on the part of the follower as to how they apply their skills and competencies; in other words, the follower has agency. The idea that followers would possess individual agency means that much of the theory about the passivity of followers can immediately be discredited, but theory that ought to be discarded very rarely is. Toward which direction the follower might apply their agency, however, is less than clear, as this would remain within their own judgment. The follower is not required to follow their nominal leader but can choose why, who and, importantly, how to follow.

This gives rise to the possibility that follower allegiances can change and flex depending on the context for opportunity in which they find themselves; consequently, the target to follow changes with agency. This gives call for serious consideration by any leader, as referring back to earlier in the chapter, the absence of followers negates the possibility of leadership. Moreover, followers possess the agency to work strategically through leaders in the course of establishing their own goals and targets. This would seem to imply that followers are not willing accomplices in the leader-follower relationship and that they are engaging in an act of 'followership' but one that is embedded within the leadership relationship itself.

There might be a danger here that practitioners and leaders seeking to improve their own practice of leadership get caught up in debates concerning who does what and how to define them, which is interesting but not very useful. However, the starting view is that followers are part of the relationship, and they have value as individuals who do the work and support the claims of leaders. Can this be framed in a way that is useful to the budding leader? Here, I think, the view expressed by Grint (1997), who suggests that leaders are figureheads propelled by events and people beyond their control, might prove useful. Just as others judge someone else's leadership, followers will make similar judgments about our own. To what extent this might be important is a call to be made by the individual, but what appears to be beyond a reasonable doubt is that leaders ignore their followers at their peril.

## Reflexive questions

Do you perceive yourself as a follower, a coworker or a leader? Why might you think this, and can you identify any limitations in the way you think about these roles?

Do you readily follow? How do you feel when following?

## Note

1  It is acknowledged that psychodynamic theories have interpreted the role of leader and follower. However, due to the scope of this book this literature will not be covered here, and the reader is directed, for a more comprehensive approach, to Gabriel, Y. (1999). *Organizations in depth*. London: Sage; Stech, E.L. (2004). Psycho-dynamic approach. In: P.G. Northouse, ed., *Leadership theory and practice*. London: Sage, 235–263.

## References

Avolio, B. (2011). *Full range leadership development*. New York: Sage.

Bass, B.M. and Avolio, B.J., eds. (1994). *Improving organizational effectiveness through transformational leadership*. New York: Sage.

Bryman, A. (1993). *Charisma and leadership in organizations*. London: Sage.

Collinson, D. (2006). Rethinking followership: A post-structuralist analysis of follower identities. *The Leadership Quarterly*, 17(2), pp. 179–189.

Empson, L. (2017). *Leading professionals: Power, politics, and prima donnas*. Oxford: Oxford University Press.

Evans, P., Hassard, J. and Hyde, P. (2013). *Critical leadership*. London: Routledge.

Greenleaf, R.K. (1970). *The servant as leader*. Cambridge, MA: Center for Applied Studies.

Grint, K., ed. (1997). *Leadership, classical, contemporary and critical approaches*. Oxford: Oxford University Press.

Jackson, B. and Parry, K. (2008). *A very short, fairly interesting and reasonably cheap book about studying leadership*. London: Sage.

Kerr, S. and Jermier, J. (1978). Substitutes for leadership: Their meaning and measurement. *Organization Behaviour and Human Performance*, 22, pp. 374–403.

Martin, R. (2012). The case and context for quality working relationships. In: C.L. Heimer-Rathbone, ed., *Ready for change? Transition through turbulence to reformation and transformation*. Palgrave Macmillan, Basingstoke, pp. 129–144.

Martin, R., Epitropaki, O., Thomas, G. and Topakas, A. (2010). A critical review of Leader-Member Relationship (LMX) research: Future prospects and directions. *International Review of Industrial and Organizational Psychology*, 25, pp. 61–91.

Meindl, J.R. (1990). On leadership: An alternative to the conventional wisdom. In: B. Staw and L. Cummings, eds., *Research in organizational behavior*. Vol. 12. Greenwich, CT: JAI Press.

# 6 Power, politics, resistance and leadership

The issues of power, politics and resistance in the workplace appear to be a particularly thorny problem. Whilst many would acknowledge the existence of all within organizational life, this is also matched with a reluctance to really engage with the issues as they affect working realities, seemingly preferring that they remain unseen. This chapter begins with a discussion about the disinclination to tackle the 'Unseen' dimensions of organization, after which a focus on the dynamics of power, politics and resistance and the implications for leadership are given. In the final part of the chapter, interrelationships of these dynamics are related in order to frame leadership in a way that incorporates rather than ignores a critical part of the working lives of organizational actors.

## Seeing the 'unseen'

Organizations possess a whole array of systems that influence individual behavior. Diagram 6.1 shows one way of thinking about them in order to understand their foundations and implications. The matrix comprises two separate continuums of formal/informal and sanctioned/unsanctioned aspects of organizations.

The first continuum is concerned with the levels of formality of the specific system of influence. French and Bell (1990)[1] pioneered the use of the metaphor of an iceberg to depict the structure of complex functioning of organizations within which the organization is seen to exist on two levels: the formal and the informal. The formal structure is apparent in the organization's operating procedures and policies, whilst the informal exists in the ways individuals both complement and circumvent the formal processes to achieve (or avoid) an objective. In some instances, despite the rationale for formal processes, they may be deemed as being obstructive when attempting to meet targets and stated performance outcomes.

To relate this back to the metaphor of the iceberg, the formal parts of the organization can clearly be seen and are therefore visible above the water-line and are apparent to all members of the organization. The informal structures of the organization therefore exist underneath the plane of visibility, beneath the water. This is not to suggest that individuals are not aware of the existence of the informal structures. The informal processes of communication reinforce not only the knowledge of both formal and informal parts of the organization but also may add to the practices that individuals employ. It is a matter of pure conjecture to consider the proportion of organizational functioning that exists above or below the water surface, as I'm fairly sure it ebbs and flows; however, the amount of the organization below the water is probably much bigger than generally acknowledged as organizations may well consider that they have captured the processes of work in formal policies and standard operating procedures, without due consideration of the informal dimension.

The second continuum here concerns sanctioned/unsanctioned activities and behavior. Sanctioned behavior relates to that condoned by the organization; it is therefore legitimate and is to be endorsed and developed. Clearly

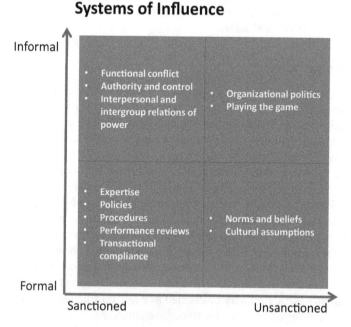

*Figure 6.1* Systems of influence in organizational life.

unsanctioned activities are the opposite, illegitimate and to be discouraged. The sanctioned/unsanctioned criteria relate more closely to issues of legitimacy and don't correspond to degrees of functionality. Following this through, when considering how systems of influence are endorsed and sanctioned by the organization, there exists a tacit acknowledgment that politics exist in the workplace but are generally considered to be something that is illegitimate, as demonstrated by the reluctance to genuinely discuss and confront it as a problem; it is a form of behavior that is not endorsed, acknowledged or developed within the workplace.

Whilst this framework is not exhaustive, it provides a heuristic device for thinking and discussing the systems contained in the organization.[2] As an example, each system of influence exerts an influence, either a required, coercive or persuasive quality upon individuals within the organization. A consideration of which systems of influence impact the individual to the greatest extent may well uncover tacit understandings about the power and political structures of the organization. Additionally, members of the organization will have different relationships to systems of influence, depending upon context, to suggest that at certain times one of the quadrants becomes more important than others. This gives rise to the possibility of the organization slipping into dissonance as one part of the organization is influenced by the formal and the sanctioned environment, whilst another operates more fully in the informal environment to influence organizational stakeholders.

This interesting observation is more fully explained by Schwartz (1990). Here the author uses two competing metaphors for the functioning of organizations – 'like clockwork' and 'like a snake pit.' The clockwork view suggests that the organization and the people within it should be appreciated as constituent parts of an extended but efficient mechanism where the agents understand their roles, expected outcomes and the way in which outcomes may be achieved; in effect, this is a textbook model of an organization, which to a greater extent is the model most would hold as their archetype for success. The alternative, which is the absolute opposite of the clockwork organization, is the snake pit. Here things fall apart, and the principle task of the agent is to ensure that it doesn't fall on them. Everyone cares, but no one seems to know what's going on. And, as people derive little joy in working with colleagues, they tend to avoid them and continue to work in silos, distanced from others. The interesting point of this is that, when asked, respondents expressed the view that they desired to work in the clockwork operation, but the organization that they knew most intimately was closer to the snake pit.

Schwartz makes a number of very interesting observations about this apparent dissonance, the most telling of which is that the quest for the clockwork against the realities of the snake pit have the capacity to significantly raise welfare concerns for members in terms of optimum effectiveness but also the possibility that work may make people ill (increased levels of stress and anxiety, leading to inappropriate behavior and consequently increased incidences of sickness and staff turnover, amongst others). Nevertheless, to bring these observations back to the consideration of the formal and informal dimensions of the organization, the clockwork is expressed in the formal/sanctioned and demonstrably desirable dimension, whilst the snake pit can be found in the informal/unsanctioned dimension below the water-line of visibility and respectability; everyone acknowledges its existence but chooses to focus upon the organizational ideal. It is the interplay that raises the possibility of how one dimension might shape the other. Does there exist the possibility that the formal dimension can be made so rigorous that it might exterminate the informal? On one hand, this seems to me to be unlikely, as experience and history suggest, but on the other, supposing we were able to do so, might the resultant clockwork organization become some form of totalistic entity that drives out all elements of individuality, expression and novelty?

From the two aforementioned continuums of criteria, the systems of influence found in organizations may be plotted, and the system of influence considered to be both informal and unsanctioned is organizational politics. There is an agreement amongst the agents of the organization that politics exists, but its very existence is almost an aberration of efficient organizational functioning – it is the gateway to the snake pit. To extend this reasoning, it has been reported by those working in organizations that their working experiences may be described as 'playing a game' but a game in which the rules are unknown. It is my argument here that the very nature of the game requires at least some competence in politics for a leader to be seen as a successful leader. In agreement with others, and in particular Heifetz (1994), whom I paraphrase here, politics at work – 'just is' – acknowledge it and learn how to deal with it. Consider this: look at your boss or their boss and determine how you would rate their political competence. Is it higher than yours?

## Sources of power

Before thinking specifically about leadership in this context, it should be noted that power and politics as influence systems are inextricably intertwined, and consequently, to discuss them in isolation is a little artificial, but that may well be necessary in order to gain a deeper understanding of the complexity. According to Hardy and Clegg (2006), organizational power has traditionally been seen as the ability to get others to do what you want, including, if necessary, against their own will, and whilst this definition of power has been challenged over the years, it's a good place to start and therefore focus is given to the founding theories where there are two diverging streams of thought. The first stream follows the work of Karl Marx (1818–1883) and Max Weber (1864–1920), where power is drawn from ownership and knowledge and is expressed explicitly as domination. The second involves the mainstream management theorists who saw the concept differently; power was not of domination but of formal, legitimate and functional authority. Resistance to this (of which there is more later) was seen as both illegitimate and dysfunctional. More contemporary work engaged in extending the ideas and concepts of the foundational theorists has really served to widen the gulf between the two interpretations.

One theorist who has attempted to bridge the gap between the two schools by providing a third dimension of power is Steven Lukes, who remains an important figure in this particular field of study. An understanding of power, according to Lukes, should not focus entirely on the observable conflicts but ought to consider questions concerning why decisions or grievances are not made – these are questions related to political quiescence – inaction as the result of power. In other words, we may be duped, manipulated or coerced into not taking a stand but entering into a state of inactivity. According to Lukes, it is this form of power that maintains the status quo and establishes the dominance of elite groupings. Additionally, this third dimension focuses on the structures of power relations that have become totally legitimized by cultural and normative assumptions. The ability to define a reality is used by dominant classes to support and justify their own material domination, which effectively heads off challenges to their own position.

The relationship of power to the conceptualization of leadership refers directly to the top ranks of the hierarchies of organization and society. I maintain that these are the leadership models to which are most frequently subscribed to become firmly established within our thinking. Might it be possible that organizational frames of leadership signed off by senior management teams are in effect models that subscribe to their own views of what constitutes leadership. After all, they are very senior and ostensibly successful, so surely, they are the exemplars of good leadership. The organizational leadership model therefore not only reinforces the position of the senior management group as good leaders but also provides a map for anyone who wishes to follow in their footsteps, regardless of whether or not the models employed here correspond in any way to actual career trajectory and behavior. This is an example of Lukes' conceptualization of the third dimension of power in evidence. In this light, advocacy of certain models can be seen as less a way to increase individual leadership and more a consolidation of the positions of the senior levels of the organizational hierarchy. In simple terms, "you all need to be like me (and I am in control)."

Furthermore, regardless of the established narratives of leadership, in effect leaders possess power, and subordinates possess less;[3] the leadership relationship is, by its very nature, unequal or asymmetrical, and again reference should be made to Smircich and Morgan (1982). The authors state that a role of the leader/manager is to provide the meaning of direction and purpose to subordinate workers. But, in fulfilling this important role, one needs to be aware that this is done from a position of power; if the manager/leader is the one who provides meaning to subordinates, this is in turn consolidates the powerful in their positions at the top of the organization, and the language of leaders is highly unlikely to be neutral. In all of the ways outlined earlier, the advocacy of leadership models and the management of meaning can be seen as illustrations of Lukes's understanding of power in organizations.

Before we leave the discussion of power, a further conceptualization related to Lukes's work but takes the third dimension one step further ought to be referred to. French philosopher/sociologist Michael Foucault's work is difficult, deliberately opaque and provocative. An understanding of Foucault's view of power starts with the Panopticon (Foucault, 1977). Nearly one hundred years before Foucault, English philosopher, Jeremy Bentham,[4] had proposed a form of prison – the Panopticon. This prison had particular qualities; for example, it was organized in a circle so that all of the cells faced the center and were completely open to view by other inmates. In the center of the circle is a tower within which the guard resides. The point here is that all members of the prison can be watched by other inmates and by the guard but are effectively unaware this is happening; consequently, the inmates behave as if they are being watched. Foucault took the implications of the Panopticon a step further to suggest that the guard doesn't require any particular skills and in effect isn't required to be present – it could be anybody fulfilling the observational role at any time and/or place. Foucault took the idea of the Panopticon beyond an institutional building and applied the theories to his observation of contemporary society.

Foucault's proposition is that individuals within society are both observing and being observed by each other, and this constitutes a form of soft power as behavior is changed and modified as a result of the observation – in Foucault's phraseology we have become disciplined. Where Foucault really adds to the understanding of power is in his assertion that individuals, as a result of observation, are complicit in their own disciplining – we discipline and are in turn disciplined by ourselves. The primary tools used in this disciplinary process are not specific actions of behavior but relate more to individual and group discourse. This establishes patterns of narratives and stories subscribed to that consequently discipline individual behavior and the behavior of others. Political activity and associated narratives constitute an element of the unsanctioned 'soft power' of the organization, but nevertheless, they shape the organization and the behavior of those within it. Leadership, in all its guises, in effect disciplines the workforce.

## Politics and the organization

Relating power to politics, Pfeiffer (1992) has stated that power reflects the exercise of influence and that political skills provides the understanding and skills to leverage the resources needed to obtain power, and establishes a relationship between the two. Nevertheless, a generalist view of 'office politics' is usually framed in pejorative language: unseemly, dishonest and self-serving. If one assumes that the backdrop for organizational functioning is rather like Schwartz's clockwork, then within such an organization there would be no need or requirement for politicking. Politics in this light may well be seen as something that is demonstrably damaging, negating the efficiency of the machine; remove it and efficiency is reestablished. I consider that this view is entirely levelheaded given the dominant view of 'efficient' organizations, founded as they are upon narratives of equilibrium economics and managerialist cost efficiencies of which even the most junior of managers will be aware. 'Levelheaded,' however, doesn't necessarily mean accurate.

A number of researchers have looked at politics in general and political skills in particular. This shift in emphasis is interesting as it implies that politicking is a skill, a competence and therefore something that can be learned and/or developed. This revitalized idea of politicking as an expertise or bundles of related competences transfers the realm of organizational politics from the unsanctioned (or even the non-sanctioned) and imbues it with at least the capacity of being seen as a fully sanctioned activity of the organization.

This view, however, is not necessarily new. In the early 1980s, Pfeffer suggested that political capability was essential for success within a political environment. Only a couple of years after Pfeffer's contribution, Mintzberg (1985) agreed that political skills were a necessary part of dealing with 'political arenas,' which is how he described organizations with an overt political nature. Furthermore, Mintzberg intimated that the political arena was an apt training ground for future leaders. He later identified more definitively the skills he had earlier generalized as necessary for exercising influence, namely, persuasion, manipulation and negotiation. The inclusion of 'manipulation' may well arouse some discomfort; however, as I have made clear throughout, the framing of leadership needs to incorporate good, bad and indifferent behavior. I consider it likely that most are aware of a leader (maybe not firsthand) who has demonstrated at least some form of manipulation to maintain or strengthen their resources of power.

Probably the most significant outline of political skill falls to Ferris et al. (2007), who have asserted that there exist four critical dimensions of competence. As the political context and the experience of the individual is likely to contribute to high levels of variability in how one might choose to deal with a situation, a clear definition of the aforementioned political skills should be considered as a work in progress. Leaving that aside for one moment, let's address the competences highlighted by Ferris and associates.

The first of these relates to *social astuteness* and the observation of others. This involves the understanding of social situations and a capacity to interpret the behavior and meanings of others. The second dimension refers to *interpersonal influence* and the adoption of a personal style that exerts an effective influence on those around them. The third dimension is defined as *networking ability* and the ability to identify and develop a wide array of contacts and networks of people; allied with this is the ability to take advantage of opportunities that emerge from the collective resources of the network. The final dimension is referred to as *apparent sincerity* in that politically skilled individuals appear to be authentic, sincere and genuine; in other words, they are able to present themselves as possessing no ulterior motives for engagement, so they can therefore be trusted because their actions are not perceived as manipulative. It is probably this dimension that evokes the same distaste brought on by the inclusion of 'manipulation.' It is the combination of these factors that promotes the ability to effectively understand others at work and to use such knowledge to influence others to act in ways that enhance one's personal and/or organizational objectives.

The consideration of power and politics with specific reference to leadership might well be a foundational part of the phenomenon that is by and large ignored. Leadership is traditionally presented in a way that assumes that leadership itself creates accord and harmony, leading to beneficial outcomes. The focus remains on the leadership, and consequently, issues of power and political relations safely can be seen as something that is outside of leadership and relegated to a dysfunctional part of the organization. There is a danger in this 'all good things' approach that is touched upon elsewhere that ought to be challenged specifically. Can a conceptualization of leadership that claims to promote harmony and consent whilst ignoring important systems of influence effectively deal with the issues of power and politics found in the organization?

## Resistance and leadership

A more critical examination of the relationships between power, politics and leadership provides us with a rationale that sees politics as normal and to be expected. Firstly, Alvesson and Sveningsson (2003) challenge the stability of leadership by considering that ambiguity exists within leadership itself. Leadership definitions in isolation are very clear, but when seen as an array of definitions, their clarity diminishes as definitions differ, different emphasis is made and consequently definitions may undermine each other. If the definition is further refined by adding subsequent elements or new definitions, the issue becomes less and less clear. Furthermore, as the definitions become less clear, the question of how to most effectively practice leadership becomes more problematic – this is ambiguity, as the application of more information does not resolve the underlying problem. Put into an organizational context where ambiguity may also exist in how one measures knowledge-based work, as an example, there exists a normalized hotbed of differences, and this is important.

The fact that individuals within an organization might be defined as leaders (and some therefore as followers) depends greatly upon their position (and resources of power) within the organization, but as a consequence of this, there is a reasonable chance that individuals may not always agree with the stated views of their nominal leader. Where there exist differences of opinion, the opportunity for potential conflict arises, and for a wide array of reasons conflict may well manifest itself in resistance. Collinson (1999), in some of his earlier work, identifies two particular resistance strategies; the first is defined as *resistance through distance*, where the individual seeks to distance themselves either physically, mentally or symbolically from the prevailing power structures of the organization, and the second is referred to as *resistance through persistence*, where employees seek to command a greater part in the running of the organization by holding managers accountable through monitoring, using information and challenging decision-making processes, such as pointing out nonconformity with the stated values as an example.

At lower levels of the organization, resistance may be seen as micro-resistances, such as not meeting deadlines or absenteeism. At the top echelons of the organization, this may constitute the ousting of a senior manager or even the CEO who falls foul of the board of directors through an act of whistleblowing. I am not attempting to paint resistance in either positive or negative terms; they may be one or the other or indeed both, but where there is difference so will there be a form of resistance in any of its many potential guises. Resistance, however, may be classified as either recalcitrant workers not doing as they are legitimately asked or as a form of power that is practiced by superordinate members of the organization. Whatever the perception, there must always exist the question as to what might be the cause of resistance, how might it be resolved and to what extent might it be acceptable.

Resistance and consent are rarely polar extremes on a continuum of practices; rather they are more often linked in contradictory ways. When considering resistance and consent within the organization, it seems to be a popular, and yet an entirely functional, view that sees resistance as either dysfunctional or nonexistent, with the latter state being the preferable one. This is where leadership, with its somewhat magical quality of rising up and joining together the aspirations of the group toward a singular goal is deemed to be important. However, the removal of resistance, or the ignorance of it, may be damaging. If the organization or significant parts of it are resisting, are their claims completely illegitimate? Could the leader be the cause or the claims of a vision, in which case it is the notion of leadership itself which is illegitimate. A leadership that acknowledges politicking and political skills therefore not only accepts the demonstration of conflict but also constitutes a path toward resolution.

Contemporary organizations are often asked to confront issues of diversity in the workplace, and this tends to focus on the acceptance of difference, whether it is of age, gender or ethnicity, amongst others. A standard view of diversity is that in essence it is to be desired, firstly, as it as it provides more favorable outcomes to the organization in terms of understanding and innovation, and secondly, being more equitable in dealing with difference is the right thing to do from a value-driven or moral perspective. Nevertheless, this is at least paradoxical from the perspective of management gaining the support of the workforce to move as one in a particular direction. As stated earlier, difference generates conflict; leaders therefore instead of relying on a kind of leadership that sees resistance as problematic, perhaps should frame the differences inherent within the system as a productive resource. And so here we have circled back to perspective, meaning and language as contributors to the resolution of leadership dilemmas and conundrums.

## Reflexive questions

Within the framework given in this chapter, where does the system of influence referred to as leadership most comfortably sit?

Reflect on the stakeholders around you. How would you summarize your political landscape?

## Notes

1 Most frequently the iceberg is used to depict the complexities of culture and climate but has been employed to illustrate all sorts of aspects of organizations, from values to cost structures.
2 It is worth considering at this point that the very way in which we have defined leadership is as a system of influence. If we were to interpose leadership as a system of influence onto the axis employed in Diagram 6.1, where would you put leadership and why?
3 I have argued elsewhere in Chapter 5, when discussing followers, that followers possess their own agency; they are not without power, but they have less than the nominal leaders within the organization. The power relationship is asymmetrical.
4 Bentham is a really interesting thinker; from the 18th century he had written extensively about a number of contemporary topics. He was a very progressive thinker, writing on diverse issues such as gender and equality, animal rights, as well as economics and money supply.

## References

Alvesson, M. and Sveningsson, S. (2003). Good visions, bad micro-management and ugly ambiguity: Contradictions of (Non-) leadership in a knowledge-intensive organization. *Organization Studies*, 24(6), pp. 961–988.

Collinson, D.L. (1999). "Surviving the rigs": Safety and surveillance on North Sea oil installations. *Organization Studies*, 20(4), pp. 579–600.

Ferris, G.R., Treadway, D.C., Perrewé, P.L., Brouer, R.L., Douglas, C. and Lux, S. (2007). Political skill in organizations. *Journal of Management*, 33, pp. 290–321.

Foucault, M. (1977). *Discipline and punish: The birth of the prison*. New York: Pantheon Books.

French, W.L. and Bell, C.H. (1990). *Organisation development: Behavioural science interventions for organisation improvement*. Englewood Cliffs, NJ: Prentice-Hall International.

Hardy, C. and Clegg, S. (2006). Some dare call it power. In: S. Clegg, C. Hardy, T.B. Lawrence, and W.R. Nord, eds., 2nd ed., *The Sage handbook of organization studies*. London: Sage.

Heifetz, R.A. (1994). *Leadership without easy answers*. Cambridge, MA: Belknap Press of Harvard University Press.

Lukes, S. (1974). *Power: A radical view*. New York: Palgrave Macmillan.

Mayes, B.T. and Allen, R.W. (1977). Toward a definition of organizational politics. *Academy of Management Review*, 2, pp. 672–678.

Mintzberg, H. (1985). The organization as a political arena. *Journal of Management Studies*, 22(2).

Pfeffer, J. (1992). *Managing with power: Politics and influence in organizations*. Boston, MA: Harvard Business School Press.

Schwartz, H.S. (1990). *Narcissistic process and corporate decay: The theory of the organizational ideal*. New York: New York University Press.

Smircich, L. and Morgan, G. (1982). Leadership: The management of meaning. *The Journal of Applied Behavioral Science*, 18(3), pp. 257–273.

# 7    Doing the right thing
## Doing things right

Throughout the book, I have been critical of how leadership in organizations is framed as an exclusively 'good thing.' In challenging this notion, two questions are broadly considered in this chapter. In the first part, the concept of good leadership itself is questioned to ask what might this comprise. In essence, is good leadership, as the title of the chapter suggests, 'doing the right thing,' or do the processes involved in 'doing the right thing' matter? Should leadership be judged exclusively by its outcomes? The second question deals with bad leadership, as there are manifestly bad leaders in the workplace. This raises questions about who exactly should be given the opportunity to lead?

### Good leadership?

The dominant framing of leadership tends to see leadership as a positive factor; frequently the solution to organizational problems is expressed as a need for more leadership. The question of how leadership might be judged as a good thing is less obvious. Is good leadership based on results, or is there an issue that relates to how those results are achieved? This dilemma is illustrated by Mintzberg (2004), who clearly criticizes managers/leaders who take deliberate actions to enhance share price despite the possibility that the exact same actions may be detrimental to the firm and other stakeholders of the firm. An example is the furor concerning General Motors, which, when facing bankruptcy in 2008, negotiated bailouts of $51 billion from which the state made a loss of approximately $12 billion. During the period from 2012–2017, the company spent over $10 billion on buying back its own stock, thus raising share price and providing a direct benefit to stockholders. Additionally, GM's values statement maintains that, "everyone feels welcomed and valued for who they are,"[1] whilst subsequently announcing that 14,000 of its employees were to be made redundant in December 2018.

The result of this is that the share price surged by an additional 5%, and this was followed by the announcement of a 4% dividend yield to stockholders, which equates to approximately 33 cents per share; the CEO owns 909,331 shares in GM and was paid in excess of $21 million in 2017. In the first quarter of 2018, GM made a net profit of $1.1 billion. How should the leadership of GM CEO Mary Barra be rated? Do the outward indicators of organizational performance tell the full story of leadership?

Let's delve into this more deeply by examining an extreme but frequently used example from Julia Ciulla, known as the "Hitler problem," which is encapsulated in a simple question: "Was Hitler a good leader?" The history of Adolf Hitler, leader of the German state between 1932 and his death in 1945, is well known, so it's not necessary to cover it here. However, Hitler took Germany from national impoverishment and the affront caused by the Versailles Treaty to become the dominant political power in mainland Europe and lead the nation into an all-but-complete military victory over the allied command by May 1940. If one was to judge his leadership by the outcomes of the state, then perhaps one might consider him to be a good leader, especially if our cutoff point was spring 1940. If, however, one takes into account the subsequent decline and the loss of the Second World War, the authoritarianism of his rule and the introduction of internal polices and genocide directed against his own people, one might consider him a very bad and 'evil' leader. But where does the balance lie? Is it sufficient to simply acknowledge the outward measures of performance, or is an account of other dimensions, including the processes of leadership, necessary when making a judgment?

It might be held that society, governed as it is by principles of freedom, individual opportunity and mobility, is an effective meritocracy, and as a consequence of this, working hard and delivering against key measures is what is required to elevate our position in society and specifically in work. Good performance equates to good leadership; leadership is demonstrated through the continued delivery of good results for which an expectation is made that career enhancement and/or benefits will follow. This appears to suggest that the results are sufficient on their own and that the process by which those results are achieved is of less importance.

It is not controversial to suggest that obtaining results by any means presents a series of inherent problems, not least that it breaks, or at least runs contrary to, the accepted wisdom of leadership as a 'good thing.' Good leadership must therefore be a combination of goal attainment delivered via processes that are complementary to the widespread expectations of good leadership. In order to consider more fully the essential processes of good leadership, the foundations provided by branches of thinking that seek to determine notions of good and bad, and right and wrong, specifically moral philosophy and ethics need to be reflected upon.

In preparation, some thought needs to be given to the differences between morals and ethics. Very simply put, morals determine what is right and wrong from an individual perspective, whereas ethics are determined by the collective, by the social grouping, be it society, the organization or family. To contemplate this overtly simplistic framing for a moment gives rise to the possibility of all sorts of complexities apparent in the determination and practices of morals and ethics; there exists a very clear possibility that they may well contradict each other. What one determines to be morally acceptable may well not be acceptable to a wider group.

In returning to the 'Hitler problem,' it is possible based upon empirical observation of the writings and speeches of Hitler to conclude that he had a very strong personal moral code. I have little doubt that Hitler believed that he was operating at the very highest moral order and that all of his actions were entirely in accordance with his moral compass. However, it should be abundantly clear when examining the actions of others sanctioned by Adolf Hitler that the vast majority of us would strongly oppose the moral correctness of Hitler's position, and, strangely in doing so, both parties could be correct. Hitler can act with moral conviction, whilst from an ethical position, the rest of society would stand in horror at those actions undertaken in the name of a greater Germany and its people. If a different example is taken, less provocative and closer to home, could it be possible for an individual to work in an ethically challenging role, say animal testing or tobacco manufacture, but morally defend their work on the basis that it provides an income that enables the individual to support their family. By extension, therefore, one might realize that operating in accordance with a moral position is not easy, as the ethics of the situation depend very much upon the subjective interpretations of the many ethical decisions imposed upon the individual. Nevertheless, and despite the fact that Hitler achieved many things, as a consequence of the processes employed, one should conclude that Hitler was very much a bad leader. It is the contention here that good leadership depends not only on one's moral position, as it is only when this is in accord with the group's ethical stance that one is able to act and make real the moral and ethical foundations of good leadership. In effect, the leader's moral compass, co-constructed through the ethics of the led, determines the direction of leadership practice.

From a leadership studies perspective the issues of ethics and leadership have not received perhaps as much attention as one might expect, and consequently, the literature is quite small. However, this should not diminish its importance, as much of the work on neo-charismatic leadership is implicitly about ethics, as the foundations of leadership as a 'good thing' resounds throughout. This perspective changes with the development of authentic leadership by Luthans and Avolio in 2003 (which is in itself an iterative development of the full range leadership theory already referred to in Chapter 2), within which the underlying moral compass informs leadership style and gives credibility to the notion of authenticity. Here neo-charismatic leadership approaches make explicit the importance of morals for the first time in the mainstream literature. Subsequently, a number of contributors have sought to demonstrate that authenticity was the essential dimension to a variety of leadership approaches and thus establish morals and ethics as the absolute necessity of leadership and, as a consequence, leadership practice.

Let us leave to one side authentic leadership to focus on the approach outlined by Ciulla (2002), which is oriented to theorizing the characteristics of ethical leadership. In the early stages of development, Ciulla deals specifically with the ethics of leadership to consider questions related to the self-control of leaders, their intentions and ability to influence outcomes, their ability to make judgments about the greater good and the moral and emotional relationships between leaders and the led. This differs from many of the other texts in this area that seek to emphasize business ethics as opposed to an ethics of leadership. Specifically, how should what is ethically distinctive in leadership, as opposed to management or any other organizational function, be established?

When people take on a leadership role, they are required to formulate relationships with others that are essentially unique, meaningful or manufactured, depending on the context, but inherent in this are characteristics that make it morally different, and this comprises the first characteristic of ethical leadership. As stated before, the relationship between leaders and the led is asymmetric; one side has more power than the other. The way power is employed therefore is constrained by the moral position of the leader; Ciulla describes this as 'moral capital,' suggesting that leaders can increase their resources of power through moral action.

The second characteristic is that the leader may have to go against their own moral position in serving different constituent groups, for example, a group of strangers or the family. Moral leaders, therefore, are required to put an emphasis on the 'duty of inclination,' the natural tendency of which for many leaders is a challenging dilemma. Altruism, it may be claimed, is the moral standard for leadership, which serves in contrast to behavior that benefits oneself at a cost to others. This is interesting as it stands against some of the prevailing logic with respect to economics, which maintains that serving one's own self-interest generates the highest social welfare and, by association, is a position of highest moral virtue. Nevertheless, examples that support either altruism or self-interest are particularly extreme; many of the cases for altruistic behavior, as examples, use the cases of Nelson Mandela or Mother Theresa, and questions ought to be raised concerning the relevance of this for grounded day-to-day leadership.

A third characteristic of ethical leadership is based upon theories of utilitarianism in that leaders have the capacity to make decisions that affect a very large group of people. However, how can leaders know what is the best decision for the greatest good for the greatest number of people? This raises the issue about standards of morality and whether those of the leader should be set higher than the rest of us. No leader has ever gotten into trouble for not having higher standards of morality. A failure to live up to either those espoused standards or the exact same standards as the rest of the group is a different question, however. Should leaders be held to account for acting on the wrong set of moral beliefs or those that are morally ignorant of the expectations of the group or both?

In recent years the outward display of a formal set of values in organizations that are to be enacted by its members has become more widely evident. In the leadership literature, it is claimed that leaders have the capacity to craft a value-based culture, and this in turn establishes expectations of ethical conduct that become the norm. In this respect therefore there is a close correspondence between ethics and values, a factor readily asserted but perhaps rarely demonstrated. There is a stream of literature that maintains values are an important part of leadership functioning, that the values of the leader reflect the values of the organization, which are transmitted (through leadership processes) to, and are accepted by, members of the organization. Values create an enduring order of beliefs concerning ways of doing things. Despite this conviction, the most extensive review of leadership, completed in 1974 by Ralph Stogdill, didn't list values as an important trait of leadership. It was not until the New Leadership thinking in the late 1970s that values were specifically included as being essential components in leadership, which adds weight to the assertion made throughout the book concerning the overstated grandiosity of the 'all is good' school of leadership.

In order to unpack the last statement, consider the potential dissonance between the usual constituents of an organization: managers and the managed. It may well be that in performing their respective roles there exists a disconnect between both groups over the allocation of resources based on the value systems that the respective populations hold. The managers of a listed pharmaceutical business may consider the allocation of resources to drive shareholder value essential. The research staff of the same business may not share this perspective and 'value' the investment in science over any other factor. In such cases, does it seem likely that any grouping of organizational values is likely to meet those of all the individuals employed by the same organization?

This apparent disconnect of values may be more frequent than acknowledged. Contemporary organizations that are 'knowledge based' are, according to Alvesson (2001), typified by heightened levels of ambiguity as a consequence of their function and environment. Claims that an ambiguous phenomenon such as leadership can resolve such ambiguity, at the very least, appear problematic. Values therefore, as a construct of leadership and, more importantly, an overarching set of values that produce a sense of consensus, seem to be at best unlikely. There exists a vast array of potential clashes related to the perception of values, such as quality over quantity, innovation over conformity, freedom over control and diversity over standardization, to list a few. The question of who sets the right values when systems of values clash is an important debate worth considering, particularly when an approach to resolve these dilemmas is to defer back to the default position as defined and established by the organization's value statement.

Copeland (2014) identified three constructs essential to value-based leadership (VBL), specifically morals, authenticity and ethics. And here it is possible to infer again the importance of the 'good' perspective informed by individual morals and collective ethics. Interestingly, authenticity is credited with the same importance, although it is completely possible to behave immorally and authentically. It is evident from the VBL literature and Copeland's review that these theories have been generated out of the failures as a consequence of the widespread promotion and application of the neo-charismatic, normative view of leadership as demonstrated by results, firm failure or the documented failures of individuals, where a lack of morals and ethics have been highlighted specifically.

In the late 20th and early 21st centuries, there have been a series of business scandals culminating in the global financial crisis, where greed and self-interest may be said to be a central motivation (amongst others) of the business leaders involved. Leading up to the crash, neo-charismatic theories have been heavily promoted and formed the central framing of leadership development programs across the developed world. The aforementioned scandals have also been shaped not by regulation or governance standards but by an apparent absence of moral and ethical standards of those in leadership positions of prominence. As a consequence, therefore, one needs to look beyond the charismatic or transformational and ensure that leaders possess strong moral and ethical standards, that they are authentic leaders. The result of this is a focus on the concept of VBL, which has grown in prominence and, along with authenticity in leadership, has become a constituent part of the dominant narrative of leadership for the early part of the 21st century.

After the financial crash and other scandals, from Enron to Volkswagen and from Facebook and Cambridge Analytica to Toyota, to name a few, perhaps some thought might be given to the actual efficacy of the models that have to date driven leadership perspective and practice. However, the empirical evidence of the systemic failure of senior leadership is theoretically countered at least by the inclusion of a moral and ethical code and the rebranding of similar theories as 'authentic.' Leaders therefore can only be truly transformational if they possess the correct moral standards.

If one accepts part of the criticism of the way leadership is framed as akin to 'do everything well' models, the requisite of being morally good can be added, which not only increases the level of complexity but also the very real chance that anyone attempting to follow this path is more likely to fail. After all, as pointed out by Pfeffer (2015), many leaders in the world of practice have 'blood on their hands' to some extent, possibly as a consequence of resolving some contentious but ambiguous dilemma in their past. Consequently, I am claiming that such individuals are extraordinarily rare and, more importantly, such a rarefied and grandiose model of leadership is perhaps the wrong one upon which to build leadership competence in the organization or wider society. Finally, one should also consider that poor performance of the firm or individual is very often attributed to a lack of leadership, and in all possibility a deficiency or a gap in the leader's makeup, including specifically morally and ethically, and so the sanctity of leadership itself is preserved and undiminished, as good leaders would not possess the alleged gaps in the first place.

## Bad leadership

In a foundational article, Jay Conger (1990, p. 1) starts as follows, "Sometimes the dark side of leadership eclipses the bright side – to the detriment of both the leader and the organization." The basic theory behind Conger's article was that the very skills that got leaders noticed in the first place can contribute to their ultimate demise if overplayed. The skills Conger refers to are strategic vision, communication skills, and impression management and general management practices. Whilst these comprise a good skillset and would potentially serve any leader well, the problems occur when the behaviors of the leader become exaggerated, they lose touch with reality and become more motivated by personal gain. In essence, the problems as outlined by Conger focus on the leader's lack of ability to see beyond their own personal perspective, an overt reliance upon a particular past record and an associated skillset that has been successful. The leader begins to believe their own history, and their individual capacity to be successful and hubris raises its head.[2]

Over a considerable period, leadership thinkers have presented charisma as being unproblematic despite evidence to the contrary. The debates about the limitations of charisma were summarized by Chamorro-Premuzic (2012).

In the article, the author lists four limitations, but as I consider the third and fourth issue to be similar I will amalgamate them to outline three principle problems. The first concerns a restatement of the view that charisma, if overplayed, obscures judgment. The difference here is that Chamorro-Premuzic refers to the impact of charm as a consequence of charisma. In essence, there are only three ways in which influence is possible: through force, through reason and through charm. Whereas force and reason are rational, charm is irrational and has more potency; however, when the charm runs out, fails or is challenged, the leader may start to rely much more on force and coercion.

The second issue deals specifically with the addictive nature of charisma, as this increases the possibility that charismatics lead their own cults, where a cult is defined as a group or movement demonstrating excessive devotion to some person, idea or thing. Tourish (2013) outlines how the most destructive manifestation of Bass's full range leadership model is replicated within cults. A cult leader possesses enormous authority in the eyes of cult members. Having invested their hopes in the leader, members are intrinsically motivated to look very favorably on the leader's words and actions. However, it is worth noting that devotion to charismatic leaders is not a new phenomenon; what is new is the application of this reasoning to the world of organizations.

The third (and fourth) dimensions relate directly to a particular literature which has been referred to as 'toxic' leadership, the popularity of which really stems from Babiak and Hare (2006). It makes some important claims that are backed up by a number of studies, including foundational studies by Robert Hare himself. The central concept of the work is that individuals with pathological psychologies are able to thrive inside contemporary corporations. Furthermore, organizations have created the context within which corporate psychopaths can rise to positions of elevated prominence. In other words, at senior levels of the organization, there is a higher incidence of clinical pathology than in the general population; there is a greater concentration of psychopaths at your place of work than in the general population.

Reference to corporate psychopaths can also be found in a complementary strand of thinking referred to as the toxic triangle; here the principle difference is that toxic leadership can be subdivided into three typologies dependent upon the pathology present. The common strand, however, is that all three types have the capacity to not only hide in plain sight and thrive but, as a consequence, may well be considered as role models for the firm. We have already met the Corporate Psychopath; the second is the Narcissist, and the third the Machiavellian. Whilst all three are distinct from each other, they do possess a similar foundation in that all three types have

an absence of empathy for their fellow man, which gives rise to their particular pathological tendencies. The psychopath doesn't acknowledge or
accept rules and behaves with disregard for the pain, mental or physical,
inflicted upon others. The narcissist is driven by a desire to feel unrequited
love and finds the kind of love they require only in themselves; their environment needs to respect and mirror this love. The Machiavellians have a
very strong desire for absolute control over themselves and others and the
activities of both.

It is interesting to note by way of an aside that alongside the 'toxic triangle' approach runs a counter approach that puts emotional intelligence at its
core. I see these approaches as the counter thesis to the toxic triangle perspective, as one is concerned with an absence of empathy, whilst the other
highlights the importance of empathy. It may well be that the incidence of
corporate pathology is quite rare, but consider the following. Have you ever
justified an action, such as restructuring to lose a problem member of staff,
disciplined someone in order to make a wider point, laid off or outsourced
work to reward shareholders, supported products that may have questionable marketing claims? A common justification for actions such as these
is often, 'it's just business', and this may well say more about individual
leaders, the organizations they work for and the kind of business that is
prevalent. The point is that pathology, as described earlier, ought to be considered as being located on a continuum; we are all a little bit pathological
in our own way.

## Reflexive questions

Think of a time when doing the right thing just didn't seem right. How did
you resolve this? What does this have to say about your leadership practice?

## Notes

1  This is a direct quote from the GM website and can be found here: www.gm.com/
   our-company/about-gm.html (Last accessed 30th March 2020).
2  There is a small but interesting literature on hubris in leadership. If you're interested, I direct you to Schlesinger, J. (1997). Fragmentation and hubris: A shaky
   basis for American leadership. *The National Interest* (49), pp. 3–9.

## References

Alvesson, M. (2001). Knowledge work: Ambiguity, image and identity. *Human
    Relations*, 54(7), pp. 863–886.
Babiak, P. and Hare, R.D. (2006). *Snakes in suits: When psychopaths go to work.*
    New York: Regan Books/Harper Collins.

Chamorro-Premuzic, T. (2012). The dark side of charisma. *Harvard Business Review*, Nov. 2012.

Ciulla, J. (2002). *The ethics of leadership*. Belmont, CA: Wadsworth Publishing.

Conger, J.A. (1990). The dark side of leadership. *Organizational Dynamics*, 19, p. 2.

Copeland, M.K. (2014). The emerging significance of values based leadership: A literature review. *International Journal of Leadership Studies*, 8(2), pp. 105–135.

Gabriel, Y. (1999). *Organizations in depth*. London: Sage.

Kets de Vries, M. (2003). *Leaders, fools and impostors*. 2nd ed. New York: iUniverse, Inc.

Luthans, F. and Avolio, B.J. (2003). Authentic leadership: A positive developmental approach. In: K.S. Cameron, J.E. Dutton, and R.E. Quinn, eds., *Positive organizational scholarship*. San Francisco: Barrett-Koehler, pp. 241–261.

Mintzberg, H. (2004). Enough leadership. *Harvard Business Review*, Nov. 2004.

Pfeffer, J. (2015). *Leadership BS: Fixing workplaces and careers one truth at a time*. New York: Harper Collins.

Stogdill, R.M. (1974). *Handbook of leadership: A survey of theory and research*. New York: Free Press.

Tourish, D. (2013). *The dark side of transformational leadership: A critical perspective*. London: Routledge.

Zaleznick, A. (2009). *The executives guide to understanding people*. New York: Palgrave Macmillan.

# 8    Becoming *leaderful*

Leadership is complicated, and in mapping out a pathway for improving practice an acknowledgment of the complexity is necessary. This chapter is divided into two parts. In the first, I will begin with a brief summary of the recurrent themes used in earlier chapters. It will prove useful to have these themes collected into a single space, and it is from these thoughts about leadership that the concept of being leaderful may be located. In the second part, an outline of the ideas and application of reflexivity is provided and used to show how leaders can become more effective when dealing with the complexity of everyday lived experiences and, in doing so, emerge full of leadership capability.

## Lead, leading, leadership. . . *leaderful*

Throughout the book, I have consistently been critical of the themes of contemporary leadership dominated by narratives of top leaders doing extraordinary things, which tend to reinforce the exalted position of leaders and their leadership. As I write this in 2020, the coronavirus pandemic sweeps the globe and an economic collapse that will dwarf the recession that followed the global financial crisis from 2008 seems inevitable. The absence of leaders rising to assault the problem suggests that the grandiose depictions of leadership, whilst legitimate in theory are not common in practice. A crisis in leadership is unlikely to be resolved by yet more leadership of the same type.

This suggests that the power of the leader is somewhat overstated in this grandiose perspective. It is not just that examples of the dominant models are rare empirically, but more that leadership of this kind alienates and renders powerless the led. It is the intention here to move toward freeing both leaders and followers so they may realize their potential within the confines of their workplaces. Leadership is important, but contemporary models typified by the 'do everything well, stable, good and authentic' (heroic) leader are flawed models that aspire to an unrealistic blueprint for practice that is more often than not likely to lead to failure and disappointment.

Organizational models of leadership wrapped up in value statements, competency frameworks and types of desirable behaviors that typify current thinking extol the virtues of the organizational equivalent of Superman. Such a task for the aspiring leader is nothing short of daunting. The problem here is that many of the models and theories are based on expectation; they are drawn from what should and ought to be. If, as an alternative, empirical examples of highly effective leaders were considered in depth at the grounded level of experience, the results of the subsequent inquiry might produce an entirely different model, but one that is achievable for the vast majority of individuals who work in our companies, public bodies, and governments. Questions concerning the attainability and practicality of leadership within our organizations should be raised and discussed as part of the process of replacing them with something more reasoned and evidence based.

Stories of leaders who are inspiring and visionary are probably more prevalent than indicated by the actual recorded case studies. Rosenzweig's use of the halo effect in the work setting is one reason why an alternative that locates leadership in the humdrum of organizational functioning should be considered. Similarly, the foundational work of Mintzberg (1973) provides a further reason to question contemporary framing. In this study Mintzberg hit upon the then radical view that in order to ascertain what managers actually do in their day-to-day work, it might be revealing to follow a group of managers around and record their actions. The results are both informative and compelling. The view of the manager as the efficient organizer, planner, forecaster, coordinator, controller and commander, as established by Taylor and others in the late 19th century, was conspicuous by their absence. In their place, Mintzberg recorded management practice as highly fragmented, contradictory, dynamic and challenging, typified by interruption and time pressures.

There are many things that can be taken away from this study, but here I will focus on just two. The first is that Mintzberg's study provides a clear empirical example of the difference between expectation and lived experience. The second insight concerns leadership directly and, given the highly fragmented nature of the work done by managers, isn't it natural to assume that the work of leaders is likely to be the same? After all, managing, leading and following are performed by the same person, just at different times. Consequently, it is an error to think of leaders and their leadership as being a stable phenomenon; their behavior is more likely to comprise some good, some bad and a lot of behavior that is unremarkable either way. In practice, leaders have better days and some that are less so. However, a tendency to see leadership as the good days only serves to construct and reinforce the collective expectations of leadership.

Alternatively, we ought therefore to think less about the isolated high-points as precedent and more about enhancing everyday practice; not only is this likely to be much more attainable by the majority but also comprises the bulk of the work performed by the individual leader. It is this that I see as being leaderful; a skilled leadership practice driven less by gestures of rhetoric and persuasion, a leadership that effectively shifts the balance of power from the top echelons of the organization's hierarchy and subsequently elevates a leadership grounded in the everyday practice of the empowered individuals who have responsibilities closer to the coalface of the organization.

## Reflecting and reflexivity

For these final pages it is my intention to speak directly to you, the reader, because this final part is specifically about you and your journey toward more effective leadership practice.

There are a number of important contributing factors of which the aspiring leader needs to be aware when embarking upon an intended program of activity aimed at becoming more leaderful.

The first issue raised concerns planning and is relatively straightforward but is critically important. It may well prove to be a mistake to reinvent yourself and attempt wholesale behavior change in order to be the effective leader that you aspire to become. In all likelihood, doing a lot of things differently is likely to leave both you and others with whom you interact confused, exhausted and, more importantly, unconvinced. In doing something differently, you will be acting against all of those patterns of behavior that you have learned over time and have, as a consequence, become your naturalized habits. As an alternative, decide upon a particular scenario for which you would wish to introduce a new element to your practice. How you might plan for this is specific to you, as what works for you may be different from what works for others; it may well be that you try a number of different strategies before you find one with which you are comfortable.

Nevertheless, be clear about what you will do differently and what the intended outcome is. This is important, as in doing something differently, the outcomes will be different, too, even if they are only subtle. If, however, the outcomes are not what you envisaged, you might well be falling into the trap of believing in your own halos. Introduce differences into your practice in measured steps, and review the outcomes before deciding what to do next. Consider also letting others know and seek their approval, as doing something new may well be a shock to those with whom you are interacting, unless they are warned. It is through repeated practice of new behaviors that they become more located within your subconscious routines to become normalized – your new habits, only more effective.

This last point leads us to consider the second issue, and that is to consolidate the processes that lead to more effective practice. The core skill here is the ability to reflect on your various experiences in order to interrogate and understand them. This is less straightforward than it first appears; both you and those involved in the experience will have perceptions about what occurred, and each of those are valid. Although we are being highly interpretive by dealing with and interrogating the subjective, the actual process is itself very conscious and deliberate. Reflection is a natural process of which you are capable and moreover currently do regularly. After an event, or at the end of the day, we may run through our mind some of the video footage we have collected about the day's activities. Although you already do this, very few of us actually pay any attention to the content. Probably, if you are running through something that didn't go too well, you might acknowledge the feeling it invokes and commit to move on quickly so as to avoid the discomfort. Reflection is the conscious acknowledgment of our videos of experience; reflexivity, on the other hand, is the critical interrogation of them. As I have explained before, I will use the term 'reflexivity' to now encompass both elements.

There are a number of reflexive models that outline the stages of this interrogation, and as far as learning and developing are concerned, all are of use, particularly if they instill in you the discipline of reflexivity. One of the most prevalent models currently in use was created by Gibbs (1988) and is known as Gibbs Reflective Cycle and comprises six separate stages. These stages are titled: Description (What happened?), Feelings (What were you thinking or feeling?), Evaluation (What was good or bad about the experience?), Analysis (What sense can you make of the experience?), Conclusion (What else could have occurred?) and Action Planning (What might you do next time?). As far as it goes, this cycle can be useful for developing leadership practice, but additional steps are required to cover the depth of truly reflexive interrogation. It is fairly usual to reflect on something at the surface level, which is primarily descriptive, and this can give some important insights and make for a very good starting point, but it can be rather functional and/or superficial.

After the initial round of questioning, it may be more valuable to move through more levels of interrogation but shift the focus of that interrogation (Alvesson and Skoldberg, 2005). In the first instance, you may reflect on what occurred, asking what part you played in the event. This is an important step, as you will most likely look for causes of an issue but fail to look at the contribution you have made. Ask yourself, when things don't go quite as you thought they would, "What was my contribution to this?"

The next important stage is to do the same again but reflect on the perspectives of others to give real consideration to your responses to those perspectives. Your third pass of interrogation may well reflect upon the hidden dimensions of power and politics, and the final round may reflect specifically on the words and language used. Your videos will come accompanied by a soundtrack; language not only creates meaning but also socially constructs our shared lived realities. The objective throughout is for you to unpack and ask fundamental questions about the assumptions that led you to either do something or believe something. When you complete this interrogation and have some answers, you will have enhanced your understanding of the experience, why and how it occurred and what contribution you made to the event happening in that way at that time. Most likely you know something new about yourself.

In order for you to do something differently, you need to challenge the basic assumption of why you behaved in a certain way in the first instance. Once this is challenged and displaced by something else, you can claim to have learned something. In other words, learning something may provoke within you a different outcome that could be a better form of practice. Consequently, you need some form of stimulus to provide the impetus to learning, and this is in essence the evidence that you have at your disposal. Throughout the book, I have put together a number of topics that introduce some of the debates in leadership practice; these are debates that have proved valuable to me in teaching leadership and running leadership development workshops and have been valuable and interesting to those with whom I have had the pleasure to work. Evidence from academia is a very useful form of evidence, but it doesn't provide all the evidence. My plea here is for you to consider the theories as metaphors in that they may say one thing, but there may well be abstractions and deficiencies within the theory that need to be taken account of; no one theory holds a monopoly on truth.

You will learn and incorporate something different into your practice, and you may judge something as progress if pragmatically doing something new delivers a better outcome; the consequence is a more effective you – if it works, it is sufficiently real to you. Of course, as a reflexive novice, it may well be that you too readily accept your progress; be reflexive and seek to test the outcomes of your own practice. Evidence can come from a whole array of sources, from books, practitioner and scholarly papers, from conversations, formal appraisals and psychometric tests; simply put, the evidence of the outcomes of your own practice is everywhere, but you must be open enough to acknowledge it and reflect upon the value contained within it.

The reflexive process is an involved one that will require a concerted effort and time. It is also a process that has no end because, as you become reflexive and your practice becomes more effective, you will have embedded reflexivity as part of your new habits; you can carry it on and into other areas of your life and continually strive to become better in all of your identities. You may feel that using your time in this way is counterproductive because it firstly diverts you from the task at hand, and secondly, it is ancillary to the job, a luxury in other words. I would counter this by pointing out that all tasks have two elements: the objective and the process. You are effectively refining the process and, secondly, as you are focusing on making the process more effective, your reflexive engagement should not be considered as a distraction from the job – it is the job.

The third issue relates to the departure point for your learning journey. Your workplace and your work are a mixture of things you can control and things that are outside of your influence. Nevertheless, the one thing exclusively under your own control is yourself and the way you practice your leadership, but how you do this is your choice. You may well have a framework of leadership at work that constitutes the 'do everything well' school of leadership thinking. Within that, there will be a mix of things that you are good at and things that you don't do so well; this is usual as you are a mix of strengths and weaknesses, and inevitably you will practice your leadership in a style that is particular to you. Traditionally, development processes require you to think about and improve those elements that you are not particularly good at; in other words, we see development as problem-solving, where you are required to resolve a deficit. There may well be good reasons why you are not particularly good at something (worth reflecting on?), and attempting to make that a strength is probably going to come with a serious cost attached in terms of struggle, mental anguish and anxiety as to whether you are making the grade. The result of extended and focused labor may well result in an improvement, but I'd hazard a guess that the weakness will always remain, relatively speaking, compared to what you are good at.

It may well be that after spending a considerable amount of time working in organizations, you have become pretty well acquainted with what you're not very good at. In worst-case scenarios, our weakness becomes the sole area for development over a period of time, and I can think of nothing more dispiriting than focusing on bringing a weakness up to the level of a relative strength. I wonder, therefore, if you know what you are good at, and if you do have an idea, how do you know that you are good at something? At the beginning of your leadership journey therefore I would strongly advocate taking a psychometric test, as this will provide you with solid evidence from which you can start to think about your own practice in depth. There are many psychometric tests available, and from experience I would strongly recommend either the DiSC test or the Hogan Assessment system, as I found both valuable in my own and other reflexive investigations.

As a counter to deficit management, I would like to propose an alternative drawn from a series of ideas known as appreciative inquiry,[1] where instead of starting from a deficit, you start from a position of relative strength. Affirmative inquiry (AI) is less a prescriptive technique and more a way of living and being within the workplace amid all its component complexities; AI therefore calls primarily for openness and is entirely coherent with the reflexive processes outlined in this chapter. Every social system has something within it that works, something that gives it life when it is at its most effective. What I'm asking you to do here is to think about a leadership event when you were at your most effective and interrogate that, as we discussed earlier, in order to ascertain what gave it, and by definition, you, life.

This might not be straightforward, and so I would encourage you to actively seek evidence in support of the core of your leadership as this is unlikely to comprise a solitary element you do well, but more an array of actions and underlying assumptions that exist within your practice. Additionally, cross-reference these with your organization's leadership model and an empirical model from which you can draw from the most effective person for whom you have worked. In triangulating all of these skills, competences, behaviors and values, you will arrive at something that is in common; this is your start point, the life of your own practice. It may be that this is sufficient, but consider that over time, in practicing increased reflexivity and understanding, you can extend this core into other areas and therefore extend your competences and skills in order to become a better, more effective leader.

At the time of writing, there is an emphasis being placed upon leadership and resilience; considering this further will help illustrate what is outlined in this chapter. Firstly, a heightened focus on resilience is clearly a consequence of the coronavirus pandemic, but many of the early papers concerning the topic date back to the global financial crisis of 2008, where resilience is really seen as the ability to bounce back from a setback. On the one hand, this is timely in that it reinforces the moral requirement of leaders to look after the wellbeing of others and themselves. On the other, it is clear that the focus and emphasis of leadership depend upon context, demonstrating that leadership itself and the requisite skills of leaders are anything but stable. Performance in the face of adversity is clearly a demonstration of resilience, but as Taleb (2007) questions, who gets the reward? Is it the convenient hero who is present and highly visible post event, or the unseen individual whose work prevented the event from occurring in the first place? Adding the requirement of resilience to the 'do everything well' framework of leadership merely heightens and further exaggerates the heroic expectations of leadership in organizations.

It is asserted that the most resilient organizations are those that demonstrate agility (Holbeche, 2018) and possess the capability to respond to continually changing environments. To an extent there is nothing new here, as organizations have always faced disruption and the need to change and will continue to do so. There is a need to acknowledge that the future cannot be known, only guessed at, and as a consequence, the organization faces a minefield of wicked problems to overcome. Clockwork organizations fixated on efficiencies, visions and values around which to conform are probably not the best archetype for an organizational system capable of cultivating and demonstrating a culture of resilience or agility. In prehistory, the human animal developed a particular response to insecurity, to an extent they showed resilience. At times of challenge, humans as social creatures create communities as a source of security against threat. This is an important social practice as far as resilience is concerned, as there is a strong implication that we have learned that resilience effectively resides in others.

The leader's response to adaptive problems is to utilize all of the resources of the group to first understand the problem (what) and then decide on an answer (how), reflexively making this the center of leadership practice. The learning organization (Senge, 1990) provides an effective alternative to which we can apply the leadership developed within this book. The learning organization comprises four specific dimensions, as follows. Firstly, leaders facilitate, they don't command or direct; this frees up leaders from having to supply the answer through commanding. Secondly, in facilitating organizational dialogue, leaders ensure that discourse moves vertically and horizontally through the organization; everyone with a vested interested in the decision-making requires that their voice be heard. Leaders use their position and resources of power to clearly consolidate meaning for individuals. Thirdly, leaders embrace the pluralistic nature of the organization to freely engage with diversity of opinion and dissent. The leadership of the organization utilizes its political resources to diplomatically harness the power of the organization through strategies of advocacy and inquiry. Fourthly, the organization encourages experimentation; leaders craft hypotheses and alternative plans based upon the core strengths of the organization. Leaders literally empower others to enact solutions whilst maintaining their own responsibility for the decisions made. They understand that no one can know the future; solutions that are ineffective are used as learning opportunities that iteratively inform the next response to the issue at hand.

82    *Becoming* leaderful

Finally, remember that any skill or process, if overplayed, may become a weakness. This is an acknowledgment that regardless of how senior you become or how practiced, in essence you will always remain an incomplete leader (Ancona et al., 2007). The point being stressed here is that when leaders appreciate that they are incomplete, they will through necessity begin to rely upon other people. It is important to acknowledge your weaknesses, but you shouldn't excuse them; you may be able to negate them or compensate for them and over time displace them with something more effective, but they are still there. Nevertheless, you, as an incomplete leader, should recognize that leadership need not be held exclusively by yourself but can be a role delivered by your team or organization. This is not a function of your own inadequacy but is a demonstration that you are ready to lead. Good luck!

## Reflexive questions

Think of a time when you have been actively reflexive. What did you learn about the scenario, and what did you learn about yourself? How might this learning be incorporated into your leadership practice to make you more effective?

## Note

1  David Cooperider and Suresh Srivasta introduced and pioneered the appreciative inquiry approach in a 1987 article titled 'Appreciative Inquiry in Organizational Life.' For more of a practical guide, however, I recommend you consider Cooperider, D., Witney, D. and Stavros, J. (2008). *The appreciative inquiry handbook.* Brunswick, OH: Crown Custom Publishing.

## References

Alvesson, M. and Skoldberg, K. (2005). *Reflexive methodology: New vistas for qualitative research.* London: Sage.
Ancona, D., Malone, T.W., Wanda, J., Orlikowski, W.J. and Senge, P.M. (2007). In praise of the incomplete leader. *Harvard Business Review,* Feb. 2007.
Cooperrider, D. and Srivastva, S. (1987). Appreciative inquiry in organizational life. In: *Research in organization change and development.* Vol. 1, p. 1.
Cooperider, D., Witney, D. and Stavros, J. (2008). *The appreciative inquiry handbook.* Brunswick, OH: Crown Custom Publishing.
Gibbs, G. (1988). *Learning by doing: A guide to teaching and learning methods.* London: Further Education Unit.
Holbeche, L. (2018). *The Agile organization.* 2nd ed. London: Kogan Page.
Mintzberg, H. (1973). *The nature of managerial work.* New York: Harper & Row.

Rosenzweig, P. (2014). *The halo effect.* 2nd ed. London: Simon & Schuster.

Senge, P.M. (1990). *The fifth discipline: The art and practice of the learning organization.* New York: Doubleday/Currency.

Taleb, N.N. (2007). *The Black Swan: The impact of the highly improbable.* New York: Random House.

### Additional sources

Argyris, C. (2011). *Organizational traps: Leadership, culture, organizational design.* Oxford: Oxford University Press.

May, T. and Perry, B. (2017). *Reflexivity: The essential guide.* London: Sage.

Schön, D.A. (1991). *The reflective practitioner.* Aldershot, Hant: Ashgate.

# Index